River Song

After reading for a degree at Somerville College, Oxford, Alison Morgan taught in a secondary modern school and a girls' grammar school for several years. Her widely praised novel *Fish* – which was serialized on BBC television – quickly established her as a major children's writer, whose books are now translated into many languages. Her novel *Pete* was the first juvenile title to receive the Welsh Arts Council Literature Prize.

Alison Morgan is married, with two sons, and leads a very full life in a village near Builth Wells in Breconshire.

Alison Morgan

River Song

text illustrations by Sally Holmes
cover illustration by Robert Howe

Piccolo Pan Books

First published in Great Britain 1976 by Chatto & Windus Ltd
This edition published 1978 by Pan Books Ltd,
Cavaye Place, London SW10 9PG

ISBN 0 330 25344 1

Made and printed in Great Britain by
Cox & Wyman Ltd, London, Reading and Fakenham

for John

Contents

1 Pied Wagtail

Oh, the blackness and the whiteness of him as he bobbed and bobbed above the water! He swayed and bowed and curtsied, and his long tail flickered up and down in the sunshine. Two beady, black eyes glanced here and there out of a bright face, snow-white against the blackness of his head and the horseshoe-shaped bib under his bill. The rippling river broke his reflection into twenty pieces of dancing white and black, like a jigsaw puzzle that somebody had pulled apart. Timothy, the pied wagtail, was looking for his dinner.

A grub floated towards the bank with the movement of the waves. Timothy watched it till it drew level with him. Then, holding his breath, he ran straight into the shallow water, clinging to the pebbles with his curved toes, so that he would not be lifted off his feet and carried away.

He ducked under the water and saw, through a strange world of rocks wavering in the green-golden water, his dinner floating not an inch away. One snap, and Timothy was back on his stone, bobbing in the sunshine as he swallowed the grub and flicked his feathers back into place.

A wren, small and mouse-like, slipped out of the grass-grown bank and, with piercing suddenness, burst into song right in Timothy's ear. Timothy leaped up with a nervous flutter of wings.

'Oh, dear, you did make me jump,' he said a little crossly, for he did not like being taken by surprise.

'Thought I'd startle you,' said the wren with a soft chuckle.

'I can't think, Richard,' said Timothy, 'where a bird as tiny as you keeps such a loud voice. I don't make such a din when I sing.' And he sang a gentle twittering tune that could hardly be heard above the rippling water.

'I like singing loud,' said the wren, and he burst into a second song.

Timothy jumped again with a flutter of black-and-white wings in the air and then hurriedly sat back on the same stone.

'Trouble with you is you're too nervous altogether,' said the wren, grinning.

Richard himself was as brave as a lion. He would fly up at cats or owls that came near his nest, shouting angrily in their faces. He was not even afraid of the big boys who strayed along the riverbank, but would slip out almost from under their feet and sing defiance at them from a nearby bush. Now he flew back to the bank, hunting for food, for his wife was brooding on a dozen tiny eggs and waiting for him to bring her something to eat. Tonight the eggs would hatch, and he would have to work still harder, but he did not mind that. He liked being busy.

Down on the shingle, Timothy bobbed in the dappled shade. A shaft of sunlight now fell upon his gleaming white, now glinted on the black, and all the time he danced along like a ball on a piece of elastic, peering and prying for little things to eat. In a flash of green and blue and chestnut, a kingfisher shot downstream with a short shriek, and Timothy leaped in the air, quivering.

As he ruffled his feathers back into place, he thought sadly, 'It's quite true: I am a very nervous bird. But somehow, when things take me by surprise, I jump. What was that?' And he was up in a flutter of pied wings, as the shadow of a passing crow fell on his patch of sunlight.

It was the last sunlight he was to see for a week. The next morning he woke early to a world of dripping green leaves. It rained all that day, and the day after, and for several days after that. By the end of the week, the river was a red, swirling monster. It had swallowed up all the shingle patches where Timothy liked to dance along, looking for food; it had crept out among the green grasses of the fields; and it sucked and gurgled around the alder roots along the bank. Timothy felt cold and unhappy. He had not been dry for a week, and the noise of the river frightened him. He decided to leave it for a time and go to a quiet farmyard he knew of.

'I'll just go and say goodbye to Richard,' he thought. 'He must be having a hard time of it feeding that great family of his in this weather. I hope his roof doesn't leak.' But he was not really worried, for he knew the wren was one of the most famous nest builders in the country.

He swooped along till he came to the place where he had last met his friend. He knew Richard had his nest in some ivy growing around the trunk of one of the trees alongside the river.

As soon as he got near, he realized something was wrong. Both Richard and his little brown wife, Ruth, were fluttering wildly up and down among the branches, shrieking at the top of their voices. Huddled up against the trunk, some five or six small, wet fledglings opened their yellow-rimmed bills and wailed with cold, hunger, and fright. But where were the others? Timothy alighted on a twig and, bobbing, bobbing in the rain, glanced about him. Yes, there were only six gaping mouths in that unhappy cluster, and he was sure Richard had told him of twelve eggs ready to hatch. Where were the others? Where was the nest?

'What's the matter?' he asked, dropping down to perch on a trailing ivy branch that dipped right into the flooded river. It was there that the wrens kept returning, running down the branch till their feet were almost in the water, then fluttering back to the babies.

'Oh, bother you,' scolded Richard. 'Get out of my way!'

But Ruth turned to him, desperately. 'Can't you do something?' she cried. 'See, see, see, my babies will be drowned!'

She turned and hovered over the cluster of ivy leaves at the far end of the branch which was tugged by the fierce current. Then Timothy saw that the other little wrens were out there, clinging to the roof of their sodden nest. The whole ivy branch in which the nest had been built had been torn from the tree in the storm and was now submerged in the river, except for the end with the bunch of leaves and the nest itself. It would not be long before they, too, would go under, or else the branch would be torn away and the little wrens would be swept away downstream.

'Do? What can he do?' muttered Richard, jumping up and down at the very edge of the water. There was no room for a bird even as small as he to perch out on the nest beside the babies, and they were too young to fly.

But there was one thing Timothy could do, timid though he was; he could walk through water, for that was the way he very often got his dinner.

He tried, now, to edge himself along the hairy strand of ivy, into the river itself. But the current swept his feet away,

and, with a flutter of wings, he leaped in the air just in time to save himself from being sucked under. He tried again, this time taking a firm grip on the stem with his long toes, as he had often done before – but never in a torrent like this. The river was like a wild animal, pushing him, pushing him; it took all his strength to resist it.

As soon as the little wrens saw help so near, they rushed at him, clinging to his back, his sides, his tail; they nearly knocked him over.

'I can't take you all at once,' he panted, holding his beak up so that water would not go down it. 'Only two.' The baby wrens were too frightened to take much notice, but Richard came to the rescue at once. Hovering overhead, he ordered the children about and hustled four of them back on to the dome of the nest. He got the other two perched securely on Timothy's back, their feet tucked down inside his wings. Then he flew alongside, giving little cries of encouragement as Timothy struggled back towards the tree-trunk.

Where the branch dipped in the centre, the water grew

deeper and the current stronger. The river began to flow over his back, washing around the legs of his frightened passengers, who wobbled about so much that Timothy could scarcely keep his balance. He ducked his head under, to see where to put his feet, but here was no world of green-golden water and wavering rocks – nothing but choking mud that got into his eyes and nostrils. He lifted his head out, gasping for air; his feet ached with the effort of clinging on against the force of the river.

Then, suddenly, he found the current getting weaker, and the water no longer reached to his shoulders. Then only his legs were washed by the eddying ripples, and at last he stood on the dry branch beside Richard and Ruth.

While they helped their babies down and led them up the bough to their brothers and sisters, Timothy just stood, his sides heaving, while muddy water streamed off his black-and-white feathers. But as soon as the second fledgling was safe, he flew back to the nest for the next trip. Now that there was room for him to land on the half-floating island, he did not have to make the journey on the tightrope both ways.

Going back the second time, carrying two more baby wrens, was hard, though, and the third time was harder still, for he was getting tired. Once he put his foot on a piece of loose bark that crumbled off and floated away down the river. Timothy gave a lurch that nearly spilled his passengers into the water, but he put up one wing to steady them, and all was well.

He was very glad to reach the dry branch for the last time and have his two friends bustling about him and asking if he was all right. He stood quite still for a minute or two, panting, with his eyes closed. Then he gave a sudden shake of his feathers, showering water all over Richard, who was watching him anxiously, and cocked one eye up at the sky.

'Why,' he said, 'it's not raining.'

The sun was shining out of a blue gap in the clouds, and the little wrens had stopped crying. They were sitting in a fluffy row, basking in the sunshine, and Ruth had already begun to feed them.

'Thanks, Timothy,' said Richard. 'If there's ever anything I can do . . . you know.'

'I'm glad I could save them,' said Timothy. 'It's a pity about your nest, though,' he added, looking at the mossy ball, now almost completely submerged. As they watched, the strand that held it broke away, and ivy, nest, and all went whirling away down the river.

'Oh, it doesn't matter about that,' said Richard. 'I always make a few spare; there's another not far away. Just needs a bit of tidying up – don't you worry – I'll soon have everything in order.'

Timothy began to bob and sway in the sun, fluffing out his feathers to dry. He stretched out first one pied wing and then the other, and preened himself.

Richard, hopping about nearby, looking for grubs to feed his family, stopped for a moment and burst into song. Timothy leaped in the air nervously, then settled again quickly, and glanced sheepishly at his friend. Richard gave a little chuckle but said nothing at all.

2 Tyce

One night, Timothy woke while it was still dark. There was no moon, only a greyness in the sky, against which the tangled twigs above him showed like black lace. Below the skyline it was all black. Peering nervously, Timothy could not tell whether he was staring at black tree-trunks close at hand or across black nothingness to the distant mountains. He shivered a little and tucked his head back under his wing. It was warmer like that and felt safer.

But he did not go back to sleep. Soon his head was up again, cocked a little to one side; he was listening in the darkness and the silence. Something had awakened him. What was there, in the still black night, which he could neither see nor hear but might be prowling around noiselessly?

Then he heard it – a faint huffling noise – very soft, very close. As Timothy listened, motionless, the tickly feeling down his back died away, and his heart, pounding beneath his breast feathers, quietened. It was only another small bird making noises in its sleep.

Timothy began to feel irritated. Whoever it was huffling in the still night was very thoughtless, waking up other birds and giving them frights, so that they were too agitated to go to sleep again. He dug his head well into the warm patch under his wing and tried to shut the noise out.

But still, by straining his ears, he could just hear it. *Huffle, huffle,* then a sort of gasp; then a small, steady huffling again.

'I won't listen,' he told himself, but very soon he found he was listening to hear whether he could still hear it if he did listen; and he could.

He took his head out again. 'Stop huffling, whoever that is,' he whispered crossly into the darkness. No bird, however cross, likes to shout in the night.

There was silence instantly. Then a little sigh, cut off in a gulp that sounded very like a sob. Then silence again.

Timothy listened until he could bear the silence no longer.

'Don't stop huffling just for me,' he murmured softly. 'I mean, you can go on if you really want to.'

'I don't want to,' said a quavery little voice. 'It'th jutht that I can't help it.' It huffled again, sadly.

'Who are you?' asked Timothy. The voice sounded very young.

'I'm Tythe,' it said. 'And I've lotht mummy.'

'Oh,' said Timothy. 'You mean Tyce?'

'Yeth.'

'You've lost your mother?'

'Yeth. And Ramthey and Binda and Teth.'

'Who are they?'

'My brother and thithterth,' said Tyce. 'And I'm not in the netht.'

He began huffling again desperately as he sensed the cold night all about him: no warm, wriggling bodies beside him and mother's downy breast above – only draughty space between him and the stars, and a bleak stick beneath his feet.

'No, I see,' said Timothy. Then he added, encouragingly, 'But big birds don't sleep in nests.'

'I know,' said Tyce, and then, after a pause, 'I'm not a very big bird.'

Silence. Then a little huffle.

'Would you like . . .' said Timothy, 'that is, would you feel better if . . . if you came and sat by me? I'm up against the tree-trunk here, and if you got between me and the trunk, you might feel better.'

'Oh, *yeth*,' said Tyce. '*Pleathe.*'

Instantly there was a scrabbling noise, and the huffling

turned to puffing. Then a voice said from quite close at hand, 'Where are you?'

'Here,' said Timothy.

Puffing again, and more scrabbling. Then the voice said, 'Where are you now?' It sounded rather trembly and came from above Timothy's head.

'Here,' said Timothy. 'I think you're above . . .'

There was a sudden muffled shriek, and bits of moss and bark fell on his head, and something at once soft and scratchy tumbled past him and clung to the branch at his feet. A blackbird in the next bush half woke up with a loud stutter of fright and then subsided into sleep again.

Timothy sorted out his toes and set Tyce on his feet.

'It ith you all right, ithn't it?' asked Tyce anxiously.

'Yes, it's me,' said Timothy, 'but you really mustn't go about making such a row in the middle of the night. You don't know who might be around – it just isn't safe.'

But he was wasting his breath. Tyce was fast asleep.

Timothy passed an uneasy night. He kept dozing off and jerking awake with sudden fright as Tyce stirred in his sleep, dimly conscious that a tree-trunk and a nervous wagtail were not as cosy as a nest full of brothers and sisters.

After the fourth time that Timothy awakened, he looked around him and thought that the sky was a lighter grey. Now he could just see the outline of the branches and the ivy leaves against the fields. He watched and waited, and excitement stirred within him.

Every morning it was the same – that mounting happiness that trembled right through him, from his beak to the tip of his elegant long tail, as the sky paled from inkiness to leaden grey, from leaden grey to silver . . . and then from behind the farm buildings, a thread of brightness shone upon the silver and turned it all to palest blue. Long before that, Timothy was on his perch, bursting himself to make his twittering song heard above the massed choir of every bird between the river and the hills. The blackbird who had stuttered so fearfully in the night was flooding the meadow with music so rich and full that all the other birds around sounded as no more than the accompaniment to his song.

Gradually the chorus subsided. One by one, small birds grew conscious of their urgent need of breakfast, and their songs broke off as they paused to think of likely spots for a good meal. Then, one after another, they hopped away to forage among the leaves, or down in the meadows and hedgerows, or on the shingle by the river.

Tyce had just woken up. He opened his eyes slowly and stretched out first one wing, and then the other, wobbling on his perch as he did so. He looked fluffed out and cold, and he stared at the trim wagtail with round, scared eyes.

'Hullo,' said Timothy. 'How do you feel this morning?'

'Wath it you,' asked Tyce, 'in the night?'

'Yes.'

'But I've never theen anyone like you. You're all black and white.' As Timothy said nothing, Tyce added hastily, 'I think it'th very thmart, but I've never theen anyone all black and white before. Are you fierthe?'

'Fierce? Me? Oh, no.' Timothy bobbed up and down with astonishment. 'It's time for breakfast,' he said, 'and I'm hungry. Are you?'

'Yeth,' said Tyce, 'oh, *yeth.*' He sat quite still on the branch and looked trustingly at Timothy.

'Oh,' said Timothy. 'Yes, I see.' He thought for a moment, scratching the back of his head. This was a problem for Richard. He had lots of children – was always having them. He would know how to cope with an orphan. Just now, though, he would have his work cut out to feed his own twelve young; there was nothing for it but to go foraging for Tyce himself.

'You stay here,' he said, 'and I'll go and see what I can find.'

'Yeth,' said Tyce happily.

In a moment, Timothy was back. 'I forgot to ask – do you eat flies and things, or seeds?'

'Oh, flieth,' said Tyce. 'At leatht, I don't know what theedth are.'

Timothy hadn't much use for seeds, either, so that was lucky. He swooped across the meadow and ran about among the stones by the river. He caught several small flies and a couple of insects, and sat upon his stone to see what else he could find. Then he discovered that his beak was empty. 'That's funny,' he said. 'Where did I put them?' He realized he was not feeling quite so hungry as he had been. 'Oh,' he said, 'I ate them.' And he started collecting again.

But he soon found the same thing kept happening. Whenever he got a good beakful, his mind wandered, and he found he had absent-mindedly swallowed Tyce's breakfast.

'It's no good,' he decided. 'As long as my inside's empty, I can't keep my beak full.' There was only one thing to do. Timothy worked very hard until he did not feel hungry any more. Then he collected a large assortment of breakfast foods and flew back across the meadow.

Tyce was still patiently waiting. Timothy left him starting his first course and flew off to collect a second and a third. Then he said hopefully, 'I expect you've had enough now.'

'I'm not quite tho hungry, thank you,' said Tyce politely, but continued to fix the wagtail with a hopeful eye.

Timothy hardened his heart. 'I think it's time we had a talk about things.'

'What thort of thingth?'

'Things like who you are, and where you come from, and what we are going to do about you.'

'I'm Tythe,' said Tyce in surprise.

'I mean what kind of bird you are. What were your parents?'

'Birdth,' said Tyce.

'Yes, I know. But what did they look like?'

'They didn't look like you,' said Tyce. Then he thought hard. 'Mummy had a comfy thort of front, and the inthide of her mouth wath pink.'

Timothy sighed. 'What was your father like?'

'He wath a poet. He made up thongth. The inthide of hith mouth wath pink too.'

'What was the rest of him like?'

'Quick,' said Tyce. 'He flew ever tho quick. That'th how Teth got left behind. We all flew from the netht yethterday, firtht daddy, then me, then Binda, then Ramthey. It felt funny at firtht, but I'm quite good at flying now. Thall I thow you?'

'Not now. What did your father look like?'

'Pleathed. But then Teth wath afraid and wouldn't come. I told her it wath quite eathy, but the wath frightened.'

'Did your father look like you?'

'I thuppothe tho,' said Tyce. 'I'm all thortth of brown, aren't I?' He looked down at himself. 'Thith bit ith quite pale, with blotcheth, and here it'th yellowy-brown, and thith bit' – he screwed his head right round to examine his back – 'ith thtreaky. Do you like me?'

'Oh, yes,' said Timothy. 'The trouble is, lots of young birds look a bit like you, but when they grow up they get quite a different suit of clothes. I think I looked quite like that when I was little.'

'Oh,' said Tyce. 'Do you think I'll look like you when I grow up?'

'No. You'll wear the same clothes as your father.'

'He didn't look like you. Not at all.'

'He didn't have a red breast, the colour of a bramble leaf in autumn?' asked Timothy.

'I don't think tho. I've never theen a bramble leaf in the autumn. I wathn't even an egg then.'

'Then you'd be a robin. Just as well you're not. They bustle so. I hope you're not a sparrow either.'

'Can't we jutht wait and thee?'

'Yes, but ...' Timothy rocked to and fro, thinking of his restless night and the way those flies had disappeared. And what would happen if a cat or an owl came near? Someone had to teach Tyce how to become a sensible, grown-up bird and ...

'I shall have to go and see a friend of mine,' he said.

'Yeth,' said Tyce. 'I'm rather hungry,' he added sadly.

'But you've only just had breakfast.'

'Yeth,' said Tyce, still more sadly.

'Don't you think, now you can fly, you're old enough to catch your own flies?'

'I *have* tried, but they're thuch jiggerty thingth. They won't wait.'

'Try scratching under leaves; that's easier for a beginner.'

'I did try, yethterday, after ... after I lotht daddy and Ramthey and Binda and ...' Tyce broke off.

'How did you lose them?' asked Timothy kindly.

'We all kept on flying from tree to tree, after daddy, and I wath in front. Then daddy flew back to look for Teth becauthe the couldn't keep up, and I went on practithing, and then I couldn't thee any of them any more. I thought I'd better go back to the netht, but I couldn't find it; I thouted and thouted, but nobody came.' Tyce sat on his bough and stared at Timothy and huffled.

'Dear me,' said Timothy. 'I'll go and find my friend. He's sure to know what to do. You see if you can find some more breakfast while I'm gone.'

'You won't be long, pleathe, will you?'

'No. You'd better not go too far away.'

'Oh, *no*,' said Tyce.

'Think of something nice; then you won't huffle.'

'What thort of thing?'

'Try and make up a song, like your father.'

Tyce appeared to be thinking about that, so Timothy

dropped off his perch and swooped quickly away in search of Richard.

If Richard was singing, he was easy to find; but when he wasn't, he slipped small and silent through the undergrowth. Timothy knew that the quickest way to get hold of him was to let himself be found, so he sat on his stone at the edge of the river and waited.

The day was cool and clear. The river bore steadily towards him, past him, and away beyond the curve of red bank behind him. Crescents of silver light followed each other up to his stone, broke up, and disappeared. Between them, Timothy saw through to the wavering brown-golden stones on the riverbed. Sometimes a school of tiny fish swept by, and Timothy cocked his head in swift interest. There were not many flies about as yet, but occasionally a biggish mosquito drifted haphazardly by with trailing legs. Timothy made a half-hearted plunge at one, missed it, and returned to his perch; but he was barely settled before he was up again in a flutter of pied wings, for Richard had exploded into song behind him.

'Looking for me?' asked Richard.

'Yes, oh yes. I've got a problem.'

'What sort of problem?'

'A hungry one,' said Timothy. He told his friend all about Tyce, how he had huffled in the night, and how he had lost his family, and how he lisped, and how much he ate; and all the time, Richard's air of amusement grew. 'And so I thought,' Timothy ended, 'I would come and see you.'

'Why me?'

'Well, you're a father and used to bringing up children, and if you've got twelve already, I thought . . . perhaps . . . one more wouldn't make much difference.'

Richard sat on his piece of driftwood and roared with laughter.

'Poor Timothy,' he said, as soon as he could speak. 'Poor Timothy.'

Timothy looked at him suspiciously. 'You may laugh,' he said, 'but it's all very well for you. You're used to that sort of thing. I'm not. Children waking in the night, needing food all the time – for someone like me, it's very worrying.' He rocked upon his stone so violently that he had to run right down the side to regain his balance. 'Most worrying,' he said, as he flipped back to the top.

'And so you thought you could pass all your worries on to me?'

'You and Ruth . . . since you've got so many . . . wouldn't you?'

'Not likely. Here's me, half your size, slaving away from dawn to dusk, and Ruth already talking about another brood – that means more nests, more eggs, more sitting on 'em, more mouths to feed, and the first batch hardly begun to earn their living. And along comes you, a healthy young bachelor with no home ties, nothing to do but idle away your days, thinking you can't manage to look after one half-grown chick . . . Come, come, you don't even have to teach it to fly. Now listen to me,' he went on briskly, 'a little responsibility will be the making of you. I know you mean well and would never harm a fly . . .' Timothy, meek and dazed as he was, couldn't help glancing up to protest at this untruth. '. . . Well, would never hurt anyone's feelings. But ask yourself seriously, what real contribution have you ever made to the welfare of the community?'

Timothy stood silent, too shattered even to think of reminding his friend that less than two weeks had passed since he had rescued half the baby wren family from drowning. But Richard remembered and coughed uncomfortably.

'Hmmm,' he said. 'I got carried away. I didn't really mean that, you know I didn't. You know why.'

'No,' said Timothy. 'It's quite true. I'm not really any use to anybody.'

'Now, don't be silly. All I meant was that here was this poor little fellow needing care and protection, and here you are, perfectly capable of giving it, and you try to get out of it.'

'Yes,' said Timothy. 'I see. I'll do my best. He's quite a good little thing. I'm very fond of him. It's just that I don't know enough about it.'

'Of course I'll help,' said Richard, now completely penitent. 'Shall we go along and see him?'

'Just a minute,' said Timothy, and he began to hunt feverishly among the stones and grasses. Richard watched, grinning, while the wagtail filled his beak with food for his charge. Then he followed him across the field.

Tyce was squatting in a small, fluffy ball on the branch. He straightened out and came hopping up when he saw Timothy, but drew back shyly at the sight of a stranger.

'Don't mind me,' said Richard. 'Eat up your breakfast.'

While Tyce ate, the wren hopped around him, examining him with bright eyes.

'H'm,' he said. 'Might be almost anything. Not a cuckoo anyway.'

'Goodness,' said Timothy. 'I hadn't thought of that. You're quite sure?'

'Too small,' said Richard, though Tyce was twice his size. 'And too well brought up. Cuckoos have no manners.'

Tyce finished his last grub, wiped his beak on the bark, said, 'Thank you,' politely, and stood waiting.

'Did you manage to catch any flies while I was away?' asked Timothy.

Tyce shook his head. 'I tried, but they were too jiggerty.'

'Make up any songs?' Timothy turned to Richard. 'His father's a poet,' he explained.

Tyce nodded, speechless.

'Let's hear it,' said Richard.

Tyce hung his head and muttered something indistinguishable.

'Speak up,' said Richard.

'It ithn't very long.'

'Never mind; say it a bit louder,' said Timothy.

Tyce tucked in his beak and whispered, 'Tythe ith nithe, but he can't catth flieth.'

'Eh?' said Richard. 'Say it a bit more slowly.'

Tyce recited, in a careful, quavery voice,

Tythe
Ith nithe,
But he can't catth flieth.

'Ah,' said Richard. 'Very good. Very promising for a youngster. You keep at it.'

'But what does it mean?' asked Timothy.

'What it says,' said Richard. 'Tyce is nice, but he can't catch Flice.'

'Who's Flice?' asked Timothy.

'One of his friends, I suppose. Who's Flice, Tyce?'

'*Flieth*,' said Tyce. 'You know. What I can't catth.'

Richard drew a deep breath. 'Flies,' he said. 'I call that a very good poem. Short and to the point. I wonder ... I suppose you couldn't be a goldfinch?'

'Why a goldfinch?' asked Timothy. He thought of that pretty bird, with the flashes of scarlet and gold on cheek and wing, and wondered why Richard should connect it with the mousy-coloured fledgling in front of them.

'Probably not,' said Richard. 'It was just the poetry that made me think of them. They're an arty lot. Seen that pair that are nesting in the farm orchard this year?'

'No.'

'Fellow's called Julian, or some such fancy name. He's the sort of chap that puts flowers in his nest.'

'*Flowers?* What for?'

'Don't ask me,' said Richard. His own nest was a beautiful work of art, round as a ball and soft and warm inside, but he would never think of putting anything as odd and unnecessary as a flower in it. Timothy thought about other birds' nests that he had seen – those shaggy tussocks in the elms where the rooks reared their quarrelsome families; the round hollows in the reeds where the mother duck brooded, bright-eyed, over large, long, green eggs; the fairy hammocks slung by the whitethroats from briar to briar.

Richard cocked a suspicious eye at him. 'Now, don't start getting silly ideas in your head,' he said.

'Well, I don't know; I don't see anything wrong with it,' said Timothy, blushing slightly under his feathers.

'There isn't anything wrong with it, exactly; it just shows you the kind of bird he is; fanciful and, in my opinion, none too clean.' Timothy looked at his own sparkling white and glossy black, and said nothing. Richard, encouraged, went on. 'There's no harm in it, I dare say; but it's all of a piece with jackdaws and magpies and the rubbishy knick-knacks they clutter up their nests with. And we all know what magpies and jackdaws are like – dirty and dishonest.' He had worked himself up into quite a temper about it, but when he saw Tyce gazing at him anxiously, he added hastily, 'Of course, he doesn't *look* a bit like a goldfinch . . .'

He broke off, for Tyce had disappeared. He flew straight off his branch, veered sharply up, right, up again, plunged straight down, swung up, and landed back on the branch with a bump, puffing. In his beak he held a large fly.

He glanced from one to the other of his audience, swallowed the fly, and recited triumphantly, 'Tythe ith nithe and he *can* . . .'

'That will do,' said Timothy. All the same, he felt rather proud of his charge.

Richard was staring at Tyce thoughtfully. 'Not a goldfinch,' he said. 'There's only one bird I've ever seen catch flies like that. Timothy sort of dives at them in passing, and I don't bother with 'em much.'

He paused to make sure that both the other birds were hanging on his words and then said, 'You're a flycatcher.'

There was silence. 'Oh,' said Tyce at last. 'Ith that all right?' And he looked anxiously at Timothy.

'Quite all right,' said Timothy. 'I like flycatchers. Sensible, quiet birds. And I'm so glad you *can* catch flies.'

'Yeth, tho am I. Thall we go and get thome lunch now?'

'A very good idea,' said Richard.

So they all flew down to the riverbank.

3 Julian

A few days later, when Tyce was almost able to do all his own flycatching, Timothy flew off down to the river for a spell. Tyce still liked to have him around for company, especially at night-time, but he had made friends with the young wren family and was playing in the bushes with them. So Timothy decided to slip off to his old haunts.

Above the riverbank, the meadow lay lush and green. A still trail of water lay along a fold in the field, ebbing gently into the river at the lower end. Here was luscious mud where the cows crossed, and insect-rich weeds, burnished buttercups, and bright forget-me-nots. Timothy was flying towards this place when a sudden movement in the ditch made him swoop up in the air and perch, teetering, on the dead branch of an oak tree. He watched intently. There it was again – the doll's-eye-blue pool of forget-me-nots in that sea of green was violently shaking up and down. Then it stopped. Then it began again. Then it stopped.

There was no wind. The other clumps of forget-me-nots were still; the kingcups stood upon their thick stems so steadily they might have been handfuls of Spanish gold flung down in the meadow. Only that one bright patch of forget-me-nots shook and bent and then was still, then shook and bent again.

Then Timothy caught a flash of white and deep red among the blue, and the flicker of gold as rich as the king-cups.

He flew down on to a broad, flat tree-stump; the shadow of his tail flicked up and down on the sun-warmed top. He was right; it was the goldfinch, Julian. He was fluttering

above the forget-me-nots, trying to hover while he nipped off a spray of blue; but every time he let his weight rest for an instant on the slender plants, they bowed down into the water, and the goldfinch flew up with angry cries, shaking bright drops from his feet and wings.

'Very pretty,' thought Timothy, 'but cross.' He swooped down to the ditch and waded out among the long grasses. Reaching up, he broke off a spray of forget-me-nots with his beak and stepped lightly ashore, where he laid the flowers down and glanced up sideways at the gaudy stranger.

'*I* wanted that,' snapped the goldfinch.

Timothy bowed and flew off to the stump. 'It's for you,' he said. 'I mean . . . I got it for you.'

The goldfinch looked taken aback. Then he hopped over to the flowers and picked them up. Then he put them down again and took another grip on them with his beak. He squinted sideways at the flowers over his own shoulder. 'It's just that blue,' he said, 'with the gold and red. You can't always get it. There's really nothing like a forget-me-not for someone of my colouring.'

'It *is* pretty,' said Timothy politely.

'Oh, yes, most flowers are *pretty*; but they need the right background to make them really striking, don't you agree?' He flew up beside Timothy and laid the spray against him. 'Now *that's* effective, too, with the black and white; austere, and yet gay too. Oh, do keep *still*.'

'I'm sorry,' said Timothy. 'If I didn't wobble, I'd fall over.'

'If I wobbled like that I'd be falling over all the time,' said the goldfinch severely. He had just picked up the spray again and was trying once more to prop it against Timothy's pied flank, when an explosion of song burst out of the tuft of grass at the foot of the stump, ending in three long hoots of laughter. A small brown shadow flitted away low across the field to the alders by the riverbank. Peals of delighted mirth hung in the air above its course, like smoke behind a steam-engine.

Timothy, who had shot up in fright, settled on a flat stone nearby, quivering with shock and embarrassment.

The goldfinch hopped after him. 'What's the fuss about?' he asked. 'It was only a wren.'

'I know,' said Timothy. 'I . . . I think I must be getting along now.'

'May I really have this?' asked the goldfinch. 'Are you sure you don't want it yourself?'

'What would I want it for?'

'Haven't you got a nest?'

'No,' said Timothy. He thought about what Richard had told him but didn't quite like to ask, in case he was wrong. 'Is that . . . I mean . . . what are you going to do with it?'

'Put it in my nest, of course,' said Julian. 'It's one of the best blues I've seen. Fleur – my wife, you know – will be pleased.'

Timothy ran down towards the ditch. 'Would you like me to get you some more?' he asked. 'It's easy for me to wade in there.'

'Good gracious, no,' said Julian. 'Do you think I want to sleep on them?'

Timothy did, so he said nothing. What else could he want them for? To save answering, he picked a small but delicious snail off the back of a kingcup leaf and ate it. Julian gave a little shudder and turned to admire his forget-me-nots.

'I must take these along home before they wilt,' he said. 'Care to come and meet the wife? She'll be so grateful.'

Timothy looked around cautiously; no one was in sight. 'Yes,' he said. 'I'd like to very much. May I bring a young friend of mine?' He could see Tyce catching flies all by himself from a tree a short distance away. He had evidently parted from the wrens and was probably hoping Timothy would turn up soon.

They flew across the meadow, Julian twittering all the time, but the other two could not catch what he said. The river lay in a broad curve on their left, lead-coloured, with streaks of silver. They rose slightly to clear a hawthorn hedge and then continued over a pink, ploughed field. Julian headed for the cluster of farm buildings on the far side. Checking speed and swinging away just short of the barn where the sparrows scratched and squabbled, he flew into an orchard. Here and there, tall pear trees showed like white clouds, but the apple trees were not yet in flower. They stood gnarled and grey, with just a touch of colour where the first buds nestled pink in clusters of half-curled leaves.

Julian glanced around to make sure no enemy was about, and gave a soft call. He was watching a movement in the branches of the next apple tree.

'That's our call,' he explained. 'My idea – when I arrive, I give a little call like that . . .' and he gave it again, '. . . and then Fleur answers. And then we know everything is all right.'

'But the hathn't anthwered,' said Tyce.

'No,' said Julian. 'She hasn't.' He sounded crestfallen, rather than alarmed. Another short flight and they could see the goldfinch, dappled in the leaf shadows, very busy indeed. She twisted and turned on quick, purposeful feet, she twined roots and wool and hair with her beak, she pressed and moulded the soft lining with her feathery breast; and indeed, Timothy thought he had seldom seen a nest at once so sturdy and so snug.

'You didn't answer my call, beloved,' said Julian reproachfully.

'Too busy,' muttered his wife, her beak full of wool. Then she glanced at Julian, sitting huffed and puffy on a twig. 'Never mind, dear, I'll try and remember another time. I think it's coming along very nicely, don't you?'

Julian still looked disappointed, and his forget-me-not spray lay forgotten along the branch at his feet. Fleur's quick glance fell on it.

'There's not much point *having* a secret sign if we don't use it,' Julian was saying.

'What it really needs now,' said Fleur, looking carefully in the opposite direction, 'is something a bit special in the way of decoration.'

Julian perked up as he remembered the forget-me-nots. 'Something like this?' he said, offering the spray to her.

Fleur turned round. 'Oh,' she said. She picked it up and twisted it round inside the rim of the nest. Then she took it out again and rearranged it so that it trailed over the side. She tried it this way and that way; when she held it against the sky, the blue flowers seemed to disappear against the blue background.

'It will be like having a little bit of sky in our nest,' she said.

Then Julian had a go at arranging the flowers and told Fleur how Timothy had picked them for him. She was very grateful and suggested he might have some ideas about how they should decorate the nest with them. Timothy had none, but the two goldfinches were much too full of ideas of their own to notice or to pay any attention to Tyce, who was fascinated by the brilliant birds.

In the end, the spray was beginning to look rather limp so they picked all the flower-heads off and stuck them round the rim of the nest. Timothy left them to it, but Tyce remained, admiring and silent.

After that, Julian often visited the trees where Timothy and Tyce lived. As he fluttered from place to place in search of seeds, he would talk endlessly about art and poetry and life, and Tyce would follow, listening. Fleur seldom appeared; she was too busy sitting on her five eggs in the nest in the apple tree.

'I'm not sure it's good for that young charge of yours to spend so much time with the goldfinch fellow,' remarked Richard, one day, to Timothy. 'Can't think what he sees in him.'

'He helps him with his poetry,' said Timothy. 'Or that's what Tyce says.'

Tyce was catching flies from a dead branch nearby, and when Richard asked him if he had made up any more poems, he said, 'Oh, yeth, lotth. Thall I thay my latht one?'

Without waiting for further encouragement, he stood gazing out towards the horizon, and in a soft, sad voice, and trying very hard not to lisp, recited,

Shadows,
Shadows,
Darkness and despair.
Alas, the heartbreak of the burning wheel.
Blue moonlight glitters in the alder trees,
And aching, aching is the void.
'Ah,' said the golden oriole,
'Havers, havers, havers.'

As soon as he had finished, he scratched one ear cheerfully and said, 'Do you like it?'

'Er . . . what does it mean?' asked Timothy.

'Julian said you muthn't think about the meaning. In the end it will jutht come to you.'

'Has it come to you, yet?'

'No, but I thought it thounded nithe and gloomy.'

'I thought it sounded hungry,' said Timothy. 'That bit about the aching void.'

'Well, I made that bit up jutht before thupper,' Tyce said.

'I'm inclined to agree with the golden oriole,' said Richard. 'Timothy, I think it's high time you found Tyce some proper flycatchers to give him his education.'

But just then Julian himself arrived.

'Ah,' he said, 'how wise you are to be tasting the joys of summer while they last.'

'Why not?' said Timothy.

'You are lucky. You have none of the cares and disappointments of us married men,' said Julian, settling down for a long chat.

'Excuse me,' said Richard, 'I must be off to feed the family.' And with a cheerful flick of the tail, he went.

'Disappointments?' asked Timothy.

'I sometimes think hatching day is the most disappointing day of one's life,' said Julian.

'Oh,' said Timothy. 'Why?'

'First,' said Julian, 'the mate; the perfect wife; then days of shared hopes and industry; then the first egg – smooth, lovely, enigmatic.'

'Whatic?'

'You don't know what's going to come out of it.'

'But . . .'

'Then,' interrupted Julian, 'another. Each day adds to the magic hoard till there, in the nest, lies a cluster of enchanted pearls. Day by day, we brood on them and dream of the beauty locked within the frail shells. And then comes the day for them to hatch.' He sighed.

'They weren't all rotten?' gasped Timothy.

'Oh, no, not one,' said Julian, with a trace of pride. Then he added, 'At least, if they were, we should have retained the splendid vision.'

'Surely you didn't want them to be rotten?'

'No,' admitted Julian. 'No. But, Timothy, have you ever *seen* a newly hatched bird?'

Timothy had and said nothing, but Tyce said, 'No. Are they lovely?'

'Naked,' said Julian. 'Squirming. Blind. Great yellow mouths, always open. Scraggy necks. Fretful.' He stared gloomily at the river.

'Does Fleur like them?' asked Timothy.

'Fleur thinks they're wonderful. Aren't women peculiar? What's more, they have to be fed. So long. Thank you for cheering me up.' He flashed his wings and was gone.

They did not see him again for some days. Then one afternoon, Fleur arrived, very worried.

'Oh, Timothy,' she said, 'I'm so glad I've found you. I've lost Julian. You haven't seen him, have you?'

'Lost him? Where?' said Timothy.

'I don't know. He's just disappeared. Since this morning, early. As it was raining, I didn't want to leave the nest – got to keep it dry – so I asked Julian to get breakfast for me and the children.'

'Doethn't he alwayth?' asked Tyce, surprised.

'Er – sometimes,' said Fleur. 'Anyway, he went off and never came back. I waited and waited and thought he must have got into conversation and forgotten the time, and when the rain eased off, I fed the children myself. But that was hours ago, and he still hasn't come back . . . Oh, Timothy, you will find him, won't you?'

'I'll try,' said Timothy.

'He isn't very clever always,' said Fleur sadly. 'I mean about commonsense sort of things. He'd stay and talk to a *cat* if the cat listened.'

'I expect we'll find him safe,' said Timothy.

'But he's been gone for ages,' said Fleur. 'Anything could have happened to him.'

Timothy knew that only too well: cats, hawks, speeding cars; but he did not say anything.

'I can't look for him far myself,' Fleur said, 'because of the children. But I've looked in all the usual food places.'

'Leave it to us,' said Timothy. 'You go back to them. We'll call by for Richard. He'll help.'

As soon as Richard heard the news, he bustled off with Timothy and Tyce to the orchard, where Fleur had returned to her young, and asked her to explain exactly where she had already looked. Then he arranged that he would search all along the far bank of the river, where his young family could help, and Timothy should work over the near side from the orchard northwards, and Tyce should go beyond the farm.

'How will we know if he'th found?' asked Tyce.

They all thought hard. 'Perhaps the jay . . .?' said Timothy doubtfully. The jay had a loud voice but was no friend to small birds.

'I don't like mixing with them, and that's a fact,' said Richard. 'Nor with any of those big birds, crows and such. You can't trust 'em.'

'Swifts,' said Fleur suddenly. 'There's a pair nesting in the barn.'

'Would they?' asked Timothy. A couple of swifts screaming across the sky could cover the whole area in less than five minutes. But swifts were strange, foreign birds. They travelled great distances at great speed, shrieking to each other in a harsh, unfamiliar language. What did they know of hedgerow birds, pottering away their lives in a few acres of pasture?

'I'll see them,' said Fleur. 'You get on with the search. And . . . thank you.'

The three birds went their separate ways, and Fleur busied herself getting her family fed. Then, after preening herself carefully, she flew over to the barn, straight to the dark hole under the eaves where the swifts hurled themselves in and out. She tapped smartly on the corrugated iron roof. It sounded very loud.

From far within came a scuffling noise. Fleur hopped down on to the ledge beneath the roof and peered in. It was dark and dirty among the dim rafters, and smelly. The scuffling continued. Fleur stood her ground.

Then out of the darkness emerged a dark and grimy face. The mother swift hobbled out into the grey half-light and stared at Fleur suspiciously.

'What do you want?' she demanded huskily.

Fleur backed away a little. 'Please,' she said, 'I want help. My mate is lost and . . .'

'Jake!' shouted the bird back down the hole, and the tin roof echoed her grating voice. 'Jake! There's a lady here wants something.'

There was more scuffling in the distance. The mother swift stared in silence at the trim figure on her doorstep.

'It's very kind of you . . .' Fleur began.

'Ain't done nothin' yet.'

A second dark head appeared beside the first. Their blackness was not a bit like Timothy's. It looked as though if you touched it, it would rub off on you – a dingy, smudgy blackness.

'Yeah?' said Jake. 'We don't want no trippers here.'

'I'm not a tripper,' said Fleur and told her story and made her request. 'Could you possibly take a message round? You can fly so fast, and your voices carry a long way and . . . But I don't want to be a nuisance.'

'Yeah,' said Jake. 'We'll do that.' He squatted on the ledge, blinking at her.

'Oh, thank you,' said Fleur.

' 'Tain't no bother,' said the mother. 'Me and Jake, we'll be out over that little patch of ground come the evening. It's nothing.'

'It's very kind of you. I'll come and let you know if there's a message. But perhaps there won't be any need,' she added, sadly.

'Liza,' said Jake, 'p'rhaps the lady would like to take a bit of somethin' for the kiddies. We keep a bit on hand most times,' and he turned back towards the dirty hole.

'She won't like our sort of food,' said Liza.

'I'm afraid I only eat seeds,' said Fleur, relieved.

'What did I tell you?' said Liza, but she didn't seem offended.

Fleur flew back to her apple tree. When she looked back, she could see the two dark heads peering out under the roof, just as she had left them.

Tyce was working across his fourth field. He was getting very tired and wished he had been given the woodlands by the river. He was not really worried, because he could not imagine how anyone as clever and confident as Julian could be in need of help, and especially the help of a young and foolish flycatcher. Yet Fleur had made that remark about Julian talking to a cat, which was odd.

Tyce stopped at the river end of his field and caught some flies and had a drink. He felt better after that and decided to explore the grounds beyond the field.

He had to fly up over a great bank of rhododendrons and found himself looking over wide lawns sloping down to the river, a copper beech tree, roses and a woman in a raincoat who was pushing a wheelbarrow. He swung round and perched on a tall chimney.

At once, four hulking sparrows settled on the ledge beside him and jostled him, their wings half-spread and beaks open, making harsh, intimidating noises. Tyce flattened himself against the chimney-pot, but they would not leave him, so he dropped off and flew away over the roofs. The sparrows shouted after him but did not pursue him.

On the other side of the house was a walled kitchen garden full of vegetables. It did not look like anything Tyce had ever seen, and he sat on the wall, hesitating. 'Perhaps the swifts will come over and say Julian has been found,' he thought. 'Or perhaps they wouldn't do it, and Julian has been safe at home for ages and ages. Suppose I go back and find out.'

Then his eye was caught by some ripening strawberries under a net. 'What are those?' he thought, and he flew down to have a look. The net spread all over the ground where the plants grew, but Tyce perched on one of the supports and peered in. 'I wouldn't mind trying one,' he said, 'but I don't think I'd like it much.' He hopped around, curious, but there appeared to be no way of getting in.

He crouched in sudden panic as the net twitched at a place where it was gathered up into a tangle. As he watched it, ready to fly off, it gave another heave, and he saw a glint of gold.

'Oh oh,' said Tyce. He went a bit closer. 'It'th me – Tythe,' he called softly.

'Oh, Tyce, help!' came a feeble voice. It was Julian.

Tyce stared at him, horror-stricken. He had never really expected to find the goldfinch or that Julian would have got himself into real trouble. And now here he was, all tied up in a net, frightened, exhausted, his feathers all awry, his bright colours dimmed in the dust.

'How . . . how long have you been here?'

'Ages,' panted Julian. 'I can't get out.'

Tyce hopped nearer, feeling rather sick. Julian was lying down, with strands of netting wrapped around his feet and his wings and his neck. He struggled briefly and then lay back with his eyes closed.

'Oh, dear,' thought Tyce. Aloud, he said, 'I mutht go and get Timothy or Richard.'

Julian opened one eye. 'Don't leave me,' he whispered huskily. 'You must help me.'

Tyce thought about the woman in the raincoat and owls and hawks and cats. 'I'll try,' he said in a quavery voice.

He pulled and tugged and untwisted and lifted, and at last it did seem as though the goldfinch was not quite so deeply entangled. But then Julian gave a weak flutter, and it all became muddled again.

'Don't *do* that,' said Tyce quite severely, and Julian subsided at once.

At first, Tyce kept glancing nervously behind him, terrified of what might find him in this strange place; but after a while, in his concentration on the net, he forgot about dangers. A sudden rustle made him start round in alarm.

It was a robin – perky, curious. 'Hullo,' he said. 'What, another?'

'Oh, pleathe, help me.'

The robin nodded and set to work straightening out the bundle of netting at his feet. 'Goldfinch, is it? That's a change. It's usually blackbirds – clumsy great creatures. You wouldn't believe how often I've done this. Pull that bit. Later on in the season it's a positive nuisance. I've had to start making a charge. Now shake – that's better. And some of them never seem to learn. There's one blackbird – hang on to that a moment – I must have rescued twenty times. Pays on the instalment system now – one worm for me every evening through the winter, and then I keep a lookout on the nets in the strawberry and cherry seasons. Now that piece.

Thanks, I've not seen you before, have I? Nor him. Strangers here? I thought so. Now, I think that's almost clear. You pull that way, and I'll lift here, and if you, sir, don't mind giving a little shake – no, don't flap the wings, gently does it . . . ah, that's right.'

'Oh, Julian!' said Tyce, as the goldfinch fell free upon the damp earth.

The robin cocked his head on one side and considered the limp creature. 'Looks a bit sorry for himself, doesn't he? Never mind; he'll soon be as right as rain.'

'What about . . .?' Tyce began timidly.

'Oh, that's all right, bless your heart. I don't charge strangers. You don't look as though you'd know one end of a worm from the other. You take the gentleman home before he gets into any more trouble.' And the robin hopped off, erect and cheerful.

'What a shattering experience,' murmured Julian, still stretched on the ground.

'Do you think you could fly a little?' begged Tyce. The garden seemed to him to be full of dangers.

'My dear Tyce. Fly? I shall be lucky if I can stand.' He did stand, all the same, and stared in a dazed way at his dishevelled feathers. 'I need a drink,' he said. 'Cool, refreshing water.'

'The river ith quite clothe,' said Tyce. 'Thith way.' He flew up to the wall before Julian had time to reply, and waited to see if he would follow. As soon as Julian fluttered weakly to the wall, Tyce was off again, over the roofs and towards the gleaming curve of the river, and once more Julian followed.

Timothy was very tired and sad. He had zigzagged to and fro over a vast area until he felt he could go no further, and had seen no sign of Julian. He knew, far better than Tyce, how likely it was that Julian would never be seen again.

There was one more meadow to look over; then he must return to the meeting-place in the orchard. He sighed and flew low along the hedge.

At that moment a great crescent shadow shot over him and then another. Timothy looked up; nothing but bulging clouds. Then the shadows swept over him again, and he heard the shrill voices. Round and back circled the two swifts, in huge arcs across the sky, screaming their message till it echoed from hillside to hillside.

Light at heart, Timothy turned and flew straight for the orchard where Fleur kept watch over her nest.

It seemed a long way for a tired wagtail. The swifts catapulted overhead once more and then vanished into nothingness.

'What grace! What speed!' thought Timothy. 'I wish I could fly like that.'

4 A Day by the Sea

'What do you say to a day at the sea?' asked Richard.

Timothy was standing in the shallow water, pecking at anything appetizing that floated past. He stared at Richard.

'The sea?' he asked.

'Yes. Why not? Do you want to be a stick-in-the-mud all your life?'

Timothy looked at his toes disappearing in the sandy bed of the river and hurriedly ran out on to the shore. 'My family,' he remarked, 'has always travelled a good bit. We are not, like wrens, limited to a field or so and a clump of trees for our ideas of the world.'

Richard chuckled. 'You needn't give yourself airs just because your great-uncle once visited Libya. *You've* never been further afield than the farmyard up-river where you were born.'

'Nor have you,' said Timothy.

'Now is the time to put that right. My first brood is independent, and the second clutch will not hatch for another week. Julian is recovered, and Tyce is now well able to look after himself. Let's have a day out.'

'How,' said Timothy, 'do you propose to get to the sea and back in a day?'

'By bus,' said Richard. 'Like the humans do. They go every year about this time. All the females.'

'Do you think I'm going to sit on a smelly, stuffy seat in a bus with a lot of female humans all around me?'

'No,' said Richard. 'Not in. Out. At the back. Come and see.'

He flew across the river and up the hedgerow till he

T–RS–C

reached a cluster of houses where two lanes met. On the edge of the village, a battered bus stood empty and silent on a patch of rough ground. The sight of it was familiar to both birds, for it was often to be seen trundling around the lanes, taking children to school or housewives to market. Once or twice a year, however, it set out on a more adventurous trip. Notices appeared on a board outside the village shop, and people gathered together in groups, discussing plans. The bus owner gave his bus its annual wash, and he spent long hours tinkering under the bonnet and examining the tyres.

'He was washing it yesterday,' said Richard. 'I saw him when I took the children up here to teach them about houses. Now, look.'

He alighted on the rear number plate and waited till Timothy joined him. The number plate did not fit against the back of the bus but was linked to it by two metal bars. There was just room for a wagtail – and plenty for a wren – to perch on these bars hidden between the back of the bus and the number plate.

'You can turn round, but I can't. My tail gets in the way,' complained Timothy.

'There's no need to turn round.'

'It's a long time to have to sit in one position. Besides, I like to be able to see all round me.' Richard liked small, low, sheltered nooks, but Timothy really preferred to be out in the open, where he could see danger before it arrived.

Then Timothy thought about the sea. Julian had been telling them about it. Since his adventure, he had been talking a good deal about his travels as he rested and watched Fleur busy in the apple boughs: tales of his autumn and winter wanderings across the breadth of England, from the salty, windy flats of East Anglia to the gorse-gold headlands of the West Country. He had painted a picture of water that stretched, blue and sparkling, to the very horizon, with no close and familiar bank upon the farther side of it, as the river had; of sands where no plants grew and which were shared by seabirds and humans; of cliffs, wet with trickling springs, and above them, a tangle of brambles, a wealth of flowers of every sort, a land of plenty for hungry birds at the right time of year.

'Just now, it would be at its best,' Julian had said wistfully. 'Fleur, dear, shall we take the family there one day soon?' Fleur nodded, her beak full of food, but Julian went on, 'She won't go, I know, until the autumn. Of course, she's quite right; the children will not be ready to make the journey. But the best of it will be over by then.'

Timothy flew up on to the roof of the bus and pecked a few flies out of the guttering. He peered over the back at Richard, who cocked his head on one side to look up at him, his eyes bright with hope.

'When do we go?' asked Timothy.

Richard turned up his tail and filled the air with a burst of song, the feathers on his throat pulsing with joy.

'We'll have a story to tell that popinjay friend of yours,' he said with deep satisfaction. 'We'll go when the bus goes, of course. It won't be long now. It's just a matter of keeping an eye open. What about Tyce? Do you want to bring him?'

'He's not old enough,' said Timothy. 'I wouldn't like the responsibility. He'll be all right here, playing with your family.'

It was about a week later, while Timothy was having a bath after his second breakfast, that Richard arrived.

'Come on,' he said. 'Quick. There are a lot of female humans collecting at the crossroads, and the driver is running the engine of his bus.'

'I'm all wet still,' objected Timothy, and then, seeing Ruth had come to watch them go, he bowed to her politely.

'Never mind, you'll dry on the bus,' said Richard.

Tyce was playing with some of Richard's young family. 'Can we all come and thee you off?' he asked.

They flew along in quite a flock and slipped into the hedge bordering the lane. Some of the passengers were gathered there on the outskirts of the village, and it seemed a safer place to join the bus than in the village itself.

'None of you children are to go out into the road. You just watch us go from here.'

'Don't mith the buth back,' said Tyce.

'Of course not,' said Richard. 'And if we do,' he added hastily, 'it will be because we have decided to take it easy and fly home by stages. In which case we may be several days.' Some of the young wrens wore anxious brown faces, and Ruth scolded a little. Just then a flicker of gold shone in the hedge, and Fleur was among them.

'Good-bye,' she called softly. 'Have a nice time. Julian sends his best wishes. I've left him with the children.'

There was a grinding of gears, and the bus came down to the crossroads and pulled up. The two travellers flipped across the road and waited while the gossiping humans clambered up – Richard low down among the tall grasses, Timothy on a farm gate. Scraps of conversation so close at hand made the wagtail nervous, but he stood his ground, bobbing rather fast.

The driver stood by the step, helping up the more elderly of the passengers. When the last one was safely inside, he pulled the sliding door across with a heavy slam, and the voices were suddenly cut off. In the silence, the birds could hear his footsteps crunching round on the gravel to the far side of the bus, then the clank of his shoes on the metal step, and another slam. Out of the silence, the huge vehicle started to roar and shudder.

'Quick!' said Richard. 'Now!' They slipped on to their private perches and clung there, breathless. 'Don't wiggle so, Timothy. You'll fall off.'

'I must; what a noise!'

'And smell.'

'Do you really think . . .?'

'We're off – hang on.'

Timothy saw the grey pebbles spurting past below him faster and faster. 'I hope I'm not sick,' he thought.

'This is really something!' shouted Richard. 'Look at that hedge go past. My goodness that was the church!' Crouched low on his perch, he suddenly started to sing; his last long notes pierced above the roar of the bus.

Timothy clung on very tightly. It wasn't really very difficult. The motion was quite pleasant, and the smell less overpowering now that they were actually moving. He peered out round the edge of the number plate and saw the dotted white line unwinding itself down the middle of the road as it measured out the miles to the sea. He twittered cautiously to himself; nothing happened, so he blew out his chest and whistled as loudly as he could. The notes fell from his beak and tore away down the road after the tape-measure line. He looked over his shoulder and caught Richard's eye. Richard winked.

The bus began to slow down and stopped. There were two more people standing by a cottage gate, waiting to be picked up.

'I'm getting up on the number plate,' said Richard. 'I can't see out from here.'

'Do you think that's safe?'

'It's all right for you. You're long enough to peep around the edge.'

He got up just before the bus rolled on again. There was one more stop, at which Timothy joined Richard on the number plate, because he was getting a crick in his neck. After that, there were no more stops. For an hour they bowled along between scented hedgerows, past gardens full of early roses, grinding up hills, bounding down them.

Sometimes a car drew up behind them and hung poised a few yards away, waiting for a chance to overtake the bus. Even Richard was alarmed the first time it happened. It seemed as though the monster were pressing up, up, until it would press them right through the back of the bus itself, and yet to fly off would mean being swept instantly into its chromium jaws. After a time, though, they got used to it.

Sometimes it happened that instead of being almost swallowed up by fast cars, the bus did the swallowing. The two birds would see the hedge on their right drawing further and further away, and the white line, instead of rolling out beyond Timothy, appeared under their feet and then away out beyond Richard. Then a dusty van or truck would slide into view, enormous, alongside them, and grow smaller and smaller in the distance. Once they passed a familiar-scented red tractor; once a flock of sheep.

'This,' said Richard, 'is grand. Are you enjoying it?'

'Yes,' said Timothy.

Suddenly the bus pulled up on a wide, gravel area in front of a biggish stone building.

'Are we there?' asked Timothy. They peered about them. There was no water anywhere in sight, only the grey house, the car park, the road, and the hedge. They heard the driver's door slam, the tread of his feet round the front of the bus, the passenger door open, and a burble of voices. The driver spoke above the other voices, and when he had finished, a happy hubbub arose, and everyone began clambering out of the bus and going into the building.

'Surely the sea isn't in there,' said Timothy.

'We'll have a look,' said Richard. His voice had lost some of its confidence.

When the last human had gone, they flew across to a windowsill and peered in. All the passengers were sitting round little tables, and a girl in a white apron was taking round cups of steaming liquid and plates of food.

'They've just stopped to eat,' said Richard. 'An excellent idea. I could do with a snack myself.'

'In *there*?' said Timothy.

'What do you take me for?' said Richard. 'A robin? Come on.'

He flew away, across the car park to a hedge, and Timothy followed. It was very hot now, and they pecked about in the leafy shade, finding plenty to eat among the scented honeysuckle flowers curling trumpet-like at the bright eye of the sun. Timothy rumpled out his feathers, so that the breeze filtered through to his skin.

'I do feel itchy,' he remarked. 'I'd like another bath.'

'Listen,' said Richard. They both stood still, heads tilted. A subdued hum and an occasional clatter of china came through the open doorway of the café. Somebody out at the back sang a few swooping bars of a popular song; a car swept by on the road. But from the other side of the hedge came a different sound – the faint, cool seep of water in grass.

Timothy hopped through and looked down at a strip of lush grass, dark in the shadow of the hedge. He dropped down, fluttered an instant seeking a place to land, and found a small, flat stone half-hidden in weeds. It was tilted slightly, one end slipping under the tiny trickle of water that flowed along the overgrown ditch. Timothy drank deeply and waded into the grass-strewn stream. He stood with the delicious coolness lapping around his feet and sighed deeply with delight. Richard was hopping through the trailing grasses just above him, making happy chirruping noises to himself. A canopy of honeysuckle curled above them.

Some time later, voices emerged from the café, and feet crunched over the gravel. The creak of the door; the driver's cheerful voice; slam. Clank on metal steps. Slam again. Stutter; rumble; roar; smell.

'Come on,' said Richard. The two birds had barely perched on the number plate before the bus lurched and was off.

'I wouldn't have minded staying there and picking up the bus on the way back,' said Timothy wistfully.

'Mightn't have stopped there. Then where'd you be? Anyway, I'm not going to miss anything.'

Talking was exhausting above the noise of the engine and the scudding tyres. They sat silently watching the unrolling white line. They dozed a little. The sun rose higher in the sky. The traffic thickened. There were more houses on each side of the road, more people, more gaudy hoardings. The bus slowed down and stopped.

'Another break,' said Richard. 'Good.' He flew off towards a plane tree growing out of a hole in the pavement. The bus lurched and moved on.

'Hey!' shouted Timothy.

Richard swung round and tore down the road after the bus. His stubby wings flickered like lightning. He came to within six inches of his perch, but the bus was gathering speed and drew away from him.

'Hurry!' shouted Timothy. 'Oh, hurry!' Richard's little brown face, wearing an anguished expression, grew steadily smaller. Doggedly he hung on his course straight down the main street of the seaside town. Vans and cars roared, bicycles whirred, humans hovered on the edges of the pavement. Richard had eyes only for the great green back of the bus, rapidly pulling away from him, and the agitated speck of black and white that bobbed above the number plate.

Then, suddenly, instead of getting smaller, the bus began to get larger again. Beyond it, a great yellow light, round like the sun, suddenly turned to ruby red; the bus hiccuped to a halt, and Richard nearly crashed head-first into the back of it.

'Hey, did you see that bird?' The loud human voice sounded almost on top of them.

'Quick,' said Timothy. 'Down here; too many people.' They crouched on their hidden perches behind the number plate, both panting hard. Richard with exhaustion, Timothy with nervousness. A shadow loomed over them for a moment, but the bus moved on again, and the shadow fell away.

'Hmmm,' said Richard, as soon as he could get his breath. 'Quite a sizeable little place, this. See those shops?'

Timothy looked at him affectionately. He knew Richard had never in his life been beyond the tiny cluster of houses that they called a village.

'Yes,' Timothy said. 'For what it is, it's quite a fair size.'

The bus slowed down again, and Timothy fixed an anxious eye on his friend. Richard carelessly scratched his ear and remarked, 'One can't get along very fast in these towns, can one?'

They turned a corner, and a new road opened out behind them, flanked on one side by tall, whitewashed buildings with verandahs, and on the other by a low wall. Everywhere, it was very bright and light; the sunlight glared on the white faces of the houses, and the air was fresh and salty.

The bus swung round once more and scrunched to a halt between two other buses. Richard caught Timothy's eye and sat tight.

Then they heard the driver get down and walk round to the passenger door, the now familiar scrape of the door, the sudden loud voices, the feet on the metal step, exclamations, and bursts of laughter.

The birds waited until the footsteps and voices had died away, then flew up on to the roof of the bus.

'Look,' said Richard. 'Isn't that it?' A group of women carrying bags was gathering on the edge of the road, waiting to cross. Beyond them, beyond the glittering cars and the low stone wall, beyond the white wooden shacks with notices posted on them, lay sparkling water, clear and level to the horizon's edge. They sat side by side on the roof of the bus and stared.

At last Timothy spoke. 'It's not what I expected. It's so big.'

'You knew it was going to be big.'

'Yes. But it's bigger when you see it.'

Richard nodded.

'All that space,' Timothy went on. 'Just water. The river looks like bits of trees and fields and mud and sky all washed together; this is different. It makes me feel all funny to look at it.'

'Come on,' said Richard. 'Let's go down to it.'

They flew over the road and sat on the roof of a white hut. Timothy looked hopefully at the belt of round stones that graded down through smaller stones into gravelly shingle and then fine, pale sand. There ought to be good food under those pebbles. The only trouble was the number of people. True, they were thicker on the sand, but a constant string of children, elderly women, and family parties hobbled over the stones towards the sand, carrying bright buckets or newspapers or knitting, or else climbed back towards the road, with fine sand clinging to their skin.

'Extraordinary, the number of people about,' muttered Richard. 'Where do they all come from? They go right up to those rocks, and if you look the other way, there are just as many – more, in fact. Look at that road running out over the water on poles. They're as thick on that as starlings on a tree.'

'There are even a few spilled into the water,' said Timothy, 'but not very far. We could go beyond them.'

Richard peered short-sightedly over the ocean. 'Nothing to sit on,' he said. 'No cover.'

Timothy watched a long blue wave unfolding a creamy ribbon along the sand. Beyond, more waves gathered themselves. And beyond them, darker lines showed where still more waves began to heave themselves out of the ocean. Further again, the depth of water engulfed the very waves. Only a tranquil sweep of ever-deepening blue stretched to where the sky itself descended with a rim of mist and shut off the infinity of water from view.

Timothy sighed – a trembling sigh. 'I must fly out and see,' he said.

'I'm not coming,' Richard answered promptly. 'I haven't taken in all that's going on here, yet. See if you can find somewhere for us to spend the day. From out there, you'll be able to see what happens beyond that road on legs and the other side of those rocks.'

Timothy swooped over the heads of the holiday crowd. When he was above the breaking surf, he fluttered a moment, undecided whether to press boldly on or land on the wet sand and think about it. The strange, salty taste in the air was very strong. Some small, nearly naked humans were digging holes nearby. Patches of sand clung to them, dark on their wet feet, pale corn colour on their fat, pink bodies. Timothy dropped to the ground and edged, bobbing, round them. He wondered what they were finding in that waterlogged hole.

Just then, one of them made a wild scoop with a wooden spade, and lumps of sand flew through the air to flap down on the hard wet shore all round Timothy. He leaped up and fled out to sea.

At first he kept close to the water. Then he glanced ahead and saw, with terror, a great green wave curling over him. With a twist and a flicker of wings, he was clear just in time; but after that he flew higher.

The sea below grew quiet as he left the shore behind him. Once he saw a shadowy fleet of fish slant beneath the water. He looked ahead; the misty rim of the sky brushed the sea as far away as ever. He looked back; the holiday-makers were no more than bright specks. He could hear only the cries of gulls and the unfamiliar sounds of a great ocean going about its business.

The saltiness and the strangeness made him breathless. Suddenly he felt the truth of Richard's remark – 'Nothing to sit on' – and he turned and raced, panic-stricken, for the shore. He did not look down until he heard childish voices again and found himself above the sand-diggers. It had taken him scarcely a minute to make the return journey, and he had forgotten to look for a good place for the two birds to spend their day. He realized that if the sea beneath him were all trees and fields, he wouldn't think of having to find something to perch on every two minutes, so he turned deliberately out over the waves again and then flew along parallel with the coast, studying the shore as he went.

Beyond the pier, the bay continued in much the same way – yellow sand, blotched with humans, and ending in a long wall running out to sea. Beyond the wall were moored boats of various kinds, all unfamiliar to the wagtail. Nothing there.

The other way – and here Timothy rose up in a joyful swoop. There was a rocky headland wearing a flaming mane of gorse. He could almost feel the hot, sweet smell of it in his nostrils, hear the hum of plundering insects. As he flew nearer, he could see ragged cliffs coloured with patches of pink thrift and valerian. Behind the headland lay an empty cove and a few seaweed-covered rocks straggling across the sand, in an untidy procession, into the sea – all cut off from the crowds by the tide. He turned and flew back to Richard.

'Well,' said Richard, 'what did you find?'

Timothy told him.

'H'm,' said his friend, 'you are feeling pleased with yourself.'

'Let's go,' said Timothy.

'In a minute. I want to show you something. I've discovered what the humans find here to eat. Come and see.' He scuttled over the roof, and Timothy, following, found they were looking down on a man in a white coat. He was handing out rounds and squares of stuff that looked like sticky mud – only it was either white or brightly coloured – to all the people who kept crowding around him.

Richard watched silently until he thought Timothy had been given time to take it all in. Then he spoke. 'Fascinating, isn't it?'

'Do you suppose he digs it out of the sand? I saw some small humans making holes in the ground down by the sea. Perhaps they were looking for some.'

'Why does he give it all away then? Why doesn't he let the other people get their own?'

'Humans do funny things. Come on.' Timothy was more interested in his vision of golden gorse than in the peculiar behaviour of the ice-cream man.

'I'm not going to miss anything,' said Richard. 'I want to try some. I've come all the way here, and if eating that stuff is what people come here to do, then I'm going to do it.'

'How? Going to ask him for some?'

'If he gets it by digging, I don't see why we shouldn't.'

'We could do some digging when we get to my secret place,' said Timothy without much enthusiasm.

'I only want to taste – just to have had it,' said Richard. With a last wistful glance at the ice-cream man, he followed Timothy across the crowded beach.

'*Everybody* else who came on the bus has got one,' he murmured. Nearly all the members of the outing were sitting on the sand, with their legs sticking out in front of them, eating ice-cream. 'Why haven't they taken their clothes off, like everybody else?' he added.

'How should I know?' called Timothy over his shoulder. 'Anyhow, those two have.' The two youngest members of the party were lying on their stomachs in swimsuits, getting bright pink between the shoulder blades.

'Oh, Timothy, look!' cried Richard bitterly. Just below them, a small boy and still smaller girl trailed along the sand behind their parents. Both children held large, creamy-white ice-cream cones.

The small girl paused in the act of licking her cone to

watch Timothy's looping flight. Richard had dropped down on to a rock, and Timothy circled round to call him on. The girl's eyes followed him round, and the cone tipped sideways, forgotten, in her hand. The next moment, the ice-cream slipped out and splattered on the sand.

The bird flickering in the sunshine was forgotten. She stood quite still and silent, staring at the mess on the sand, large tears rolling down fat cheeks. Then a great hole opened in the middle of the pink face and let out a loud roar of despair.

Timothy flew down beside Richard. 'Why doesn't she pick it up?' he asked, distressed.

'There'd be *some* left even if she did,' muttered Richard, his beady eye fixed on the white splash.

The big humans had turned. The howling competed with

crooning noises for a while, then subsided to a whimper. The father led the girl across the sand towards another ice-cream man, and the woman and boy continued slowly on their way.

'They haven't even touched it,' whispered Richard. 'Look at it – all rich and white and . . . Come on.' He scurried over and stopped a few inches from the feast. Then he hopped round it. The creamy stuff glistened in the sunshine. The centre was rounded, pure, liquid-coated. The edges trickled through the sand grains.

Richard hopped nearer. It did not move but just lay there, oozing in the sun. Richard lunged forward, plunged his beak into it, and flipped back to a safe distance, all in one move. Timothy watched, a little behind.

'O-Oh!' said Richard. Then, 'Oh,' he said. Then, 'Ugh!' And he wiped his beak again and again on the salty sand.

'Not nice?'

'Ghastly. Vile. You try some.' Richard wiped his beak again. 'You won't like it,' he added, as Timothy zigzagged towards the liquid mess.

Timothy dipped cautiously into the very edge, where the melting cream disappeared into the sand. Then he snapped his beak to get rid of the grit. Then he dipped right into the squashy centre.

'Cold,' he said. 'Rather refreshing on a day like this, I think.' He tried some more. 'A bit too sweet. Unusual, though.' He took some more. 'Rather delicious. Hmmm. Definitely an acquired taste. You try some more.' He dug away busily, his feet puddling in the sticky patch.

'Timothy, you're disgusting. I'm not going to look at you.' Richard turned his back and hopped towards the rock, where he poked about in the seaweed. Every now and then he muttered, 'Ugh,' to himself, as he remembered the taste.

Once he looked cautiously round. The white mound had disappeared. Timothy was pecking at a sticky patch of sand. Richard turned away again, hurriedly.

'Timothy, you'll be sick.'

'Just coming,' said Timothy rather thickly. But he did not come at once. Richard was just about to say that he wasn't going to wait any longer, when a black-and-white figure ran up beside him. 'I've had enough now,' it said in rather subdued tones. 'Shall we go on?'

They flew along the bay. The cliffs looked higher, the gorse glowed brighter, the voices of the holiday-makers dropped away behind them. Up and over, and down into the gorse overlooking the secret cove. Richard glanced around with satisfaction. Usually he found it difficult to keep up with Timothy on a long flight. But he must be feeling very fit today, for Timothy arrived after him and seemed strained.

'This is wonderful,' said Richard. 'I could do with a good

meal. Do you realize we haven't eaten anything since the bus stopped all those miles away?'

'I have,' said Timothy.

'That muck? I don't call that food,' said Richard, and he began to hop among the gorse bushes and dry grass. Trails of creeping convolvulus and clumps of valerian hung over the cliff, and the wren slipped down little crevices and along sheltered wet ledges under their cover. He was busy for a long time.

'That's better,' he said at last and looked around for Timothy. Timothy was sitting exactly where Richard had left him. He had sunk down on the gorse and fluffed out his feathers so that he seemed to grow round his perch like a disconsolate ball. His shoulders were hunched, his eyes closed, and his tail dropped limply.

'Timothy,' said Richard softly. 'Aren't you feeling well?' The wagtail opened one eye and shut it again quickly. He said nothing.

'I expect it's that bus journey. You're over-tired. Let me get you something to eat – a good, juicy mosquito or one of those appetizing little sea snails.'

'No,' said Timothy.

'Too rich? There's a nest of fine spiders just over there. How about a few of those?'

'Please,' said Timothy, 'don't talk. Or if you must talk, don't talk about food.' He hunched down still further.

'Oh,' said Richard. 'It's like that, is it?' He cocked his head on one side and considered his unhappy friend for a minute or two. Then he thought that perhaps he had room for just another spider or two himself. From the ledge where they clustered, he could see the blue waves crawling up the sand far below.

'That's another thing,' he thought. 'Paddling; they were all doing it. I must try that.' He slipped diagonally down the face of the cliff, now flying, now hopping over jutting rock.

Then he flew low across the beach, stopping often to peck at a leathery strip of seaweed or examine a shell-encrusted boulder shipwrecked in the sand. Out to sea, the waves reared enormous heads between him and the sky, but nearer in they bowed themselves and slid quiet and flat along the sand. Richard got closer, following an ebbing wave, till he felt the wet sand trickling between his toes, sucked after the retreating waters. Suddenly a low, tawny shelf of water swept up towards him, and he leaped away in panic and landed well back up the beach. Then he moved down again, to await the next wave.

After the same thing had happened three times, he decided he had paddled enough. He flew back and pottered about among the rocks that tumbled slantwise at the foot of the cliff. Running up a gable of stone, he found himself looking down into a rock-pool, green, cool. Fronds of seaweed swayed in the water, and tiny, transparent shrimps, busy as ants, darted across the bed of sand, only to sink lazily down after each spurt. Blue-black mussels, limpets grey as dirty sheep's wool, and translucent sea snails bloomed upon the yellow floor; the encircling rock was encrusted with barnacles, rusty-brown where the salt air had stained their chalky tents. A crab jerked across the bottom; the shrimps scattered before it, the weeds eddied over it. Richard watched the strange world, a little frightened.

A shadow swung across the pool, and Timothy danced on a nearby rock. He looked sleek and smooth and gay. All his troubles were forgotten.

'There you are,' he said. 'Found anything interesting?'

'Come and look at this,' said Richard.

The hours passed; the sun swung round and filled their cove with shimmering gold. It sank towards the further headland, and fingers of blue shadow crept across the sand. On the crest of the cliff, the gorse still flamed, and Timothy and Richard fed and pottered, pottered and fed.

But down on the big bay, shadows crept too, and gently swept the holiday-makers from the sand and across the road, back to their homes and boarding-houses. Only a group of female humans remained, determined, like the birds, to make the most of their day out. Richard and Timothy took turns to fly over to that side of the headland and report.

At last Timothy came back to say they were on the move. Almost at the same moment, the rim of the sun settled on the ocean's edge, visible from the cliff-top over the back of the next headland.

'They'll take a long time yet,' said Richard. 'I want to see the sun go down into the sea. I don't want to miss anything.'

'If you're not careful,' said Timothy, 'you'll miss the bus.'

Timothy was wrong, though. They had time to watch the red globe become a semi-circle, and then a low arc of fire, then the merest sliver, then slide away and fill the water with a purplish glow, before the dawdling women had all left the beach.

Back in the car park, their bus was the only one left. The driver leaned contentedly against the sea wall, smoking a pipe and joking with his passengers as one by one they climbed the steps from the beach. The birds waited quietly on the hut till all were aboard, and then as the driver mounted his step, they slipped to their perches behind the number plate.

'Think I'll stay here for the homeward trip,' said Timothy sleepily. 'It'll soon be too dark to see anything, anyway.'

By the time they had left behind the lighted streets of the seaside town, a number of tousled heads nodded in the rows of seats with the motion of the bus, and in the cool evening air, two small birds, feathers fluffed out and heads tucked beneath their wings, rocked peacefully behind the number plate. Only the driver, vigilant at his wheel, steered his lighted ship across the hills.

They did not stop on the way back until it was time to let out the first passengers. The interruption woke the dozing birds and women, and from then on a soft hum of conversation drifted out into the still evening.

They were soon at the crossroads. The driver jumped down, trod along the gravelled verge, and pulled back the door. Creaking steps, soft voices, dying away down the four dusky roads. Richard and Timothy flew to the hedge and waited till the great creature stuttered and roared its way home.

When it had gone, the air was very still. Pale stars glimmered in a pale sky. The fields looked grey and featureless as the sea but hemmed in by the darker grey of the hedgerows. In the silence, a dog barked as some seaside reveller knocked for her dozing husband to come and open the door.

'It's been a jolly day,' whispered Richard.

'Ssh,' said Timothy.

The river gleamed in front of them. Mouse and sparrow, bat and swallow, all slept. They slipped into the alder clump in guilty silence. This was Richard's home; Timothy roosted in an ivy-clothed oak a little upstream. Tyce, he knew, would be sleeping up against the trunk, aware even in sleep that his companion was missing.

'Home again,' murmured Richard. 'Goodnight, old chap. We'll go again next year.'

'Goodnight,' called Timothy under his breath.

A silver moon crept over the hill and turned the river's ripples to black and silver. Black and silver against the ripples, Timothy flew quietly home.

5 Tyce Makes Friends

Ssparrows, sstarlings, sswifts, and sswallows
Make their nesstss in dirty hollowss,

recited Tyce carefully. All the young wrens applauded. While Richard and Timothy were away on their great expedition, and Ruth was busy sitting on the next clutch of eggs, the first wren family had decided it was time Tyce was cured of his lisp. They suggested all the words they could think of that had lots of *s*'s in them, and Tyce made them up into rhymes to help himself remember them. He was making excellent progress, but they had been at it all morning, and now everybody was hungry.

The young wrens began hopping about along the river-bank, looking for dinner, but Tyce did not join them. He knew where he wanted to spend the afternoon.

He flew away from the river, across the fields and towards the gap in the hills where the lane ran through.

He murmured as he flew,

Sixty-seven sticklebacks
And a silver snail
Sat upon a solemn sheep
And sang a silent scale.

'It's not the sort of poem Julian would like,' he thought, 'and Timothy would ask what it meant.' But then it is not always easy to make up a poem that is both beautiful and sensible when you have to make it out of words suggested to you by other people.

He had reached the double hedge that guarded the lane. This was the boundary of his world since he had come to live with Timothy, but once, long ago it seemed now, when he was very young, he had crossed that lane when he had lost the rest of his family. Somewhere on the other side, he knew, was the nest where he had been born.

'The lane' was always spoken of by adult birds as – not exactly forbidden ground, but undesirable for young fledglings. 'Of course, it's all right if you know what you're doing,' they said. 'One of these days we'll teach you all about it,' they said. Among themselves they talked about it in quite familiar terms – a place where they met for a good feed or a sunbathe, but not, definitely not, a place to take the family. Tyce had not been near it until today, when he had gone to see Timothy off, and even then he had not flown into it or across it.

The crossroads where the bus had stopped was a good deal lower down, nearer the river, than the point at which Tyce joined it now. Here it was beginning to leave the pastureland behind and climb up into open hill country.

Tyce perched on a spray in the hedge. The lane lay below him, quiet, crooked, dirty. Some sparrows and chaffinches hopped about in the ditch.

He took a deep breath and flew across to the other side. Nothing happened.

He soared out at a fly, doubled back after it down the middle of the lane, caught it, returned to his branch, and ate it. Still the lane slept beneath him. A moth wavered about between the hedgerows. Tyce swooped down and chased it a few yards, turned aside at a bluebottle, and once more returned to his perch. Somewhere a long way away, a horn sounded. The sparrows continued to squat idly on the road. Tyce dropped down after another fly.

Suddenly the monster was upon him. He shot down the road, zigzagging to the left and right. The great black-and-silver beast hurtled after him. A gust of hot air, a frightful blare of the horn, a flash of glass and burning metal, a storm of dust and a choking smell – and the lane was still once more. As the dust eddied to the ground, Tyce, gasping in the hedgerow, saw the sparrows and chaffinches still pecking about by the ditch.

'Oh,' said Tyce, 'I think I'd better get away from here.'

Beyond the lane, a ragged field sloped up towards the mountains, just as Tyce had remembered it. Short bracken fronds uncurled at the upper edge, and the hawthorn trees sometimes cut off the field from the hillside, sometimes gave way to a tumbledown wall.

The big white fallen tree that Tyce remembered was there. Its roots, dry and up-ended, were in shadow beneath the hawthorn; the naked boughs gleamed in sunshine. Tyce sat on a spike; the wood was hard and warm beneath his toes. Flies buzzed in the bracken or walked glossily over the bleached trunk.

Tyce had a leisurely meal, twittering to himself in between courses.

Oh, shy and smiling spider,
Spinning slender string . . .

He couldn't finish that one, so after a pause for flycatching, he started again.

A squirrel, a spider, a shrimp, and a shrew
Subsisted on shavings and slept in a shoe.

That did not make much sense either, but it went with a swing, and Tyce found himself repeating it over and over again. He was not catching so many flies now; for one thing, he missed seeing a good many because his eyes kept shutting.

The sun was really very hot. 'Subsisted on shavings and . . .' Tyce slept.

He was awakened by voices. 'Oh, come *on*.' 'Don't be silly – it's not far.' 'There's nothing frightening about the *lane*. Everybody flies there.' 'I'm going to, even if you're not. It looks lovely over the other side. Come *on.*' 'Hullo, who's that sitting on our stump?'

Tyce opened his eyes. Perching on a bare bough above him were two small speckled birds; a third squatted on the trunk, looking flustered.

'Tess,' said Tyce. 'And Ramsey and Binda.'

'That's Tyce,' said Tess.

'Don't be silly,' said Ramsey. 'Tyce disappeared ages ago.'

'He got run over,' said Binda. 'Or eaten by a cat,' she added gloomily.

'It's Tyce.'

'Tyce couldn't say his *s*'s,' said Binda.

'I can now,' said Tyce.

Tess went on staring at him. 'I know it's Tyce,' she said.

Ramsey and Binda looked him up and down doubtfully. 'Are you?' they said.

'Of course I'm Tyce. I should have thought you'd have known your own brother.'

'I did,' said Tess, but no one took any notice. Ramsey and Binda flew all round Tyce, examining him; then they perched one on each side of him.

'I catch all my own flies now,' said Ramsey. 'Do you?'

'Of course.'

'When did you stop lisping?' asked Binda.

'Oh, ages ago.'

'What happened after you got lost?' asked Tess.

'Oh, I found some food and somewhere to sleep. One soon makes friends, you know. Wagtails and wrens and such-like.'

'We were just thinking, Binda and I,' said Ramsey, 'of slipping across the lane to have a look at that huge river over there. Would you like to come with us, or would it be too far for you?'

'I live there,' said Tyce.

'Right down by the river?' asked Binda.

'The other side of the lane?' asked Tess.

'It's no distance. I got to know all of this valley a long time ago. I had to rescue a friend of mine – a goldfinch, a brilliant fellow, really – but he got into trouble with some nets at that big house down the other end of the valley. It was lucky for him that I found him. Lots of cats about, and so on.' He flew out and caught a fly.

There was a longish silence. Then Ramsey said, 'We had a good look at that tractor when it came up here to load hay, didn't we Binda?'

'Oh, tractors,' said Tyce. 'They couldn't catch a butterfly. Cars are much more surprising. I had quite an exciting race with one this morning.'

'Who won?' asked Binda.

Tyce considered. 'I did. At least, I think so.'

Tess shuffled up shyly. 'Weren't you very lonely that first night by yourself?'

'Lonely?' said Tyce. 'Lonely? No, of course not. That is ... of course, it was a bit chilly, and ... sort of strange; but then I met Timothy.'

He told them about Timothy, and Richard, and Julian and Fleur, the river, the orchard, and the farmyard. Binda and Ramsey told him about their lives, spent where the hills joined the fields, about sheep, and crows, and rabbits, and the harmless wheeling buzzard.

'Mother laid an egg this morning,' said Tess. 'She's going to have another family.'

'In our nest?' asked Tyce.

'No, they've built a new one,' said Ramsey. 'Come and see.'

They flew off to the wall and showed Tyce the new nest, with one egg in it, tucked into a hollow where a stone had fallen out. They had not been there long before both parent flycatchers appeared. Naturally they were pleased and excited to see Tyce again, but they seemed to have other things on their minds and soon hustled the children away. 'We can't have you all hanging about here,' explained Father Flycatcher. 'It worries your mother. It draws too much attention to the place.'

Once the first egg has been laid in a new nest, it becomes a very private place, for it has got to be kept hidden from any possible enemies for several weeks. The young flycatchers understood this and flew off.

They took Tyce across the field to a straggle of trees and showed him the nest where they had all been born. Tyce

thought it looked very small and untidy. 'Of course, nobody ever sleeps there now,' said Ramsey.

They flew on, but Tess stayed behind for a moment. She picked out one or two fallen leaves, straightened a trailing wisp of grass, and looked longingly at the forlorn home. 'It *was* a cosy place,' she whispered.

Then she flew after the others.

They had gathered at the edge of the lane.

'It's easy,' said Tyce. 'Look.' And he flipped across. Ramsey and Binda followed him. Tess wobbled on her green bush.

'I think I'll stay here,' she said.

'It's quite safe,' said Binda.

'There's nothing coming,' said Ramsey.

'Not if you're quick,' said Tyce, for he thought he detected a far-off rumbling.

'Shut your eyes and jump,' said Ramsey. 'Come on.'

Tess shut her eyes and jumped. At the same moment, a milk lorry rattled round the corner filling the lane from hedge to hedge.

'Stop!' yelled Tyce, but Tess heard nothing but the beating of her own heart and a strange roaring noise. She knew better than to look down when she opened her eyes. Instead she kept them fixed on a high branch ahead of her, where she decided she must land. Wings flickering, a look of determination on her face, she hurled herself straight across.

Something shiny and vast flashed six inches below her. A curious gust of wind made her veer in her course, and a lot of dust seemed to appear from nowhere, but Tess saw nothing but the branch ahead of her. She plumped on to it, panting slightly.

She was surprised, when she recovered her breath, to see that her brothers and sisters were still waiting for her. Usually as soon as she caught up with them, they raced on again. This time, they were all grouped round her, staring at her.

'What a noisy place,' she said. 'Shall we go on?' She turned to Tyce. 'Does the lane always roar and puff at you when you cross it?' she asked. It looked very peaceful now.

'That wasn't the lane,' said Tyce. 'That was a lorry.'

'Lorry?' said Tess. 'Lorry?'

'What did you think it was? A bus?' asked Ramsey.

'Yes,' said Tess. 'Yes, that's what I thought.'

Silently they flew on down to the river.

Tyce spent the rest of the afternoon showing his favourite haunts to his brother and sisters, and introducing them to his friends. He took them to meet the young wrens first, and then led them to the orchard where they found Julian, who talked away about migratory instincts in birds and the effect of a warm climate upon character; and the young flycatchers listened respectfully.

Then Fleur appeared and took them to see her babies in the nest.

Fleur's family had reached the stage when it was quite impossible to keep the whereabouts of the nest a secret, for the young birds were lively and growing fast, and shouting for food all day long. However, they would soon be ready to fly. In the meantime, Fleur always had to be on hand, keeping danger at bay as well as feeding the hungry family.

Binda and Ramsey wandered away after a time and found the swifts' hole. They sat on the roof of the barn and watched the dusky pair hurtling in and out, but Tess stayed with Fleur and helped her look after the children.

When the shadows of the alder trees stretched beyond the shingle and danced on the water, Binda said it was time they went home.

'Good-bye,' said Tyce. 'Come over again soon and you'll be able to meet Timothy.'

'Aren't you coming?' asked Binda.

'Where?' said Tyce.

'Home.'

'I *am* home. This is where I sleep – on that branch there, up against the trunk, and Timothy next to me.'

'We all sleep together in a row,' said Ramsey.

'When it's cold, we huddle together,' said Binda, 'and Ramsey and I whisper, and Father tells us to hush. Whoever wakes first in the morning hops out on the wall and begins to sing, and the rest all join in. Usually it's me.'

'It's me more usually,' said Ramsey.

'Once it was me,' said Tess. 'A big drop of water from a leaf fell down my neck and woke me up.'

'Come with us, Tyce,' said Binda. 'Then we'd all be together again.'

'No,' said Tyce. 'Timothy would be lonely coming back in the dark and finding no me. Besides, this is home. I couldn't sleep unless I heard the river gurgling through the night.'

'Goodnight, then,' said Binda. And they all said goodnight, and the three of them flew back up towards the lane.

In the quiet, the gurgling of the river suddenly seemed louder. Tyce pecked about and settled himself for the night. Then he sang a solitary evening twitter and settled down on his perch to sleep.

It was draughty without Timothy. The trees made much more noise than usual – strange creaks and groans – and the boughs swayed about, casting black shadows which made him cower down in fright, thinking an owl loomed over him. The river, instead of rippling steadily, would become quite silent, as though it had stopped flowing, or run away down the valley, leaving a dry bed. Then it would start sucking and plopping very loudly, with a swish of eddying currents, and Tyce would bounce out of his sleeping ball, expecting to see waves curling over his head. But still the river slipped away silvery beneath him, and the black reflections bobbed on the ripples.

'Timothy's very late,' he thought, and he envied the warm huddle of flycatchers up on the hillside. Should he try and find his way there in the near dark? But then Timothy would return and find the perch empty.

He peered out. The hills were black now, against a clear green rim of sky. Only the bats wheeled and squeaked eerily. A shape whistled past, and then another. Tyce crouched in alarm. But as they wheeled back, ebony against the diamond water, he saw they were only the swifts making their last flight before shuffling down their murky passageway to bed.

The bats merged into the darkening sky, and the swifts and swallows were gone. Downstream, a moorhen cried out in sudden panic, and a duck quacked and rustled from the bank. Then all was still.

Tyce tucked his head back under his wing and tried not to feel the empty space where Timothy should have been. Up on the edge of the hill, Tess woke with a jump and felt the lorry hurtle once more beneath her feet, but Mother Flycatcher muttered at her crossly, and she fell asleep again.

The green rim beyond the mountains turned to grey. The bats, moth-full, hung themselves up by their toes; the moorhen dreamed of counting chicks endlessly and never getting the same answer; down in the alder clump, twelve gypsy-brown wrens rose and fell in the rhythmic breathing of sleep.

'When Timothy comes home, I'll be able to tell him that I don't lisp any more,' Tyce thought. '*When* he comes home . . .'

To drive out disquieting thoughts, he began to recite to himself, very softly, all the words the wrens had been making him say. The words came slower and slower, and after a time stopped altogether.

Between the flickering shadows slipped a flickering shape; it alighted and swayed up and down on the bough near Tyce; then it edged along until it was right beside him.

'I'm back,' whispered Timothy. 'Are you asleep?'

'Yeth,' murmured Tyce.

6 The Party

For some weeks, the valley had echoed with noisy machines, shouting children, barking dogs, and was filled with the scent of new-mown hay. Then the hay was gone, leaving shaven meadows where the curlew and plover tried to hide their young from the watchful crows. Next the golden fleece of corn swayed and fell in one field after another, and Timothy and his friends ran about among the stubble on a carpet of scarlet pimpernel.

Up on the sloping hillside, the tractors got busy again, and cartloads of turnips creaked down the lane. Large, bare squares of ploughed land began to appear, and after the screaming seagulls had passed on, the little birds ran about the furrows and found plenty to eat.

The trees drooped beneath heavy overcoats. A patch of rust appeared on the chestnut tree by the farmyard. Timothy saw it and looked around at the other trees. Then he saw that all the green was dull and tired, and here and there tongues of flame, sparks of red, a scorch of brown running out to a fiery golden rim were preparing to burn up the summer foliage. Soon it would be ablaze, in the gorgeous bonfire of autumn; then bare branches, bleak winds, the cold, cold winter.

The sky darkened and sang as if with a great wind when a flock of starlings, wing-tip to wing-tip, swept down the valley and swung into the curve of the river to join up with a still larger cloud of their fellows. They wheeled and rolled themselves out on the water meadows like a magic carpet. No longer graceful, they squawked and squattered and squabbled all over the green grass.

Timothy had not seen much of Julian and Fleur for some time. They had moved upstream to join clans of their relatives. The swifts, too, swept across the sky in great companies, and the swallows twittered endlessly on the telephone wires.

Timothy sighed and went downstream to find Richard.

'It's autumn,' he said. 'Everyone is going again.'

'I think we should have a party,' said Richard.

'A farewell party?' Timothy cheered up.

'That's what I thought. We'll invite Fleur, and that silly husband of hers, and Tyce's family, and the swifts. How about having it tomorrow?'

'That's a good idea,' said Timothy. 'Have you seen Tyce? He's not been about much lately.'

'Here I am,' said Tyce, diving down among the trees. 'Been busy with family preparations.'

'We're going to have a party,' said Richard.

'To say good-bye to all our friends. They'll be going away soon for the winter,' said Timothy.

'I know,' said Tyce. 'I'm going too.'

'Of course,' said Richard. 'I hadn't thought of that.'

Timothy stared. 'You can't go,' he said. 'They go thousands of miles. It isn't like just going to the sea, and that's far enough, even if you do go by bus.'

'I've got to go,' said Tyce. 'All of our family do.'

'Didn't your mother have a second brood?' asked Richard. 'They'll be scarcely fledged yet.'

Timothy, who knew about it, looked upset, but Tyce just said, 'Oh, the eggs never hatched. The jay got them.' Life was too full of adventure and dangers to worry too much about the fate of un-hatched eggs. 'Mother pined for a day or two, but she soon cheered up. After all, she's got us.'

'But you're too young and small,' said Timothy. 'You've never even been outside this valley.'

'I've never wanted to, until now,' said Tyce. 'We'll all be going together: Father, Mother, Binda, and Ramsey – even Tess. I'm not small; even the warblers go, and they're much smaller than me.'

'He's quite right,' said Richard. 'You must just get used to the idea, Timothy.'

'Aren't you frightened, Tyce?' asked Timothy.

Tyce considered a moment. 'I hadn't thought about it,' he said. 'It's just one of those things. Every flycatcher does it.'

Timothy stared out across the river. Willows grew in an untidy clump above the earth cliff hollowed out by the current. Beyond lay the water meadow, a line of lush grass marking the course of a ditch. Above the furthest hedge he could see huddled farm roofs, and beside the hedge, apple sprays arched under a crop of reddish apples. Beyond that lay the lane and the hills, and beyond them, the windswept clouds of autumn.

'There's an awful lot of world,' he said. 'Do you think you'll ever find your way back again?'

Tyce was busy catching a fly. 'I expect so,' he said, when he had swallowed it. 'Why don't you come too?'

Out of the corner of his eye, Timothy saw Richard's anxious, perked-up face.

'Would you go, Richard?' he asked.

'I don't mind seeing a bit of the world,' said Richard, 'but I'd never sleep a night away from here. Besides, I'm not made for long flights. Bus for me.' He hopped on to a favourite log of driftwood. 'You go, and tell me about it when you come back.'

He looked ruffled, and pecked away busily in a dry and barren crack.

Tyce said, 'Come on, Timothy; come with us.'

Timothy was watching Richard's fidgety tail. 'One day I might,' he said. 'But not this year.' He swayed silently above the water, looking at his own reflection. 'Well,' he said at last, 'what about this party?'

Tyce swung round in the middle of a chase, and Richard stopped pretending to look for food.

'First,' he said, 'we must work out a programme.'

'Doesn't food come first?' asked Tyce.

'Food comes into the programme,' said Richard firmly.

'Whereabouts?'

'That's one of the things we have to decide.'

'First, I think,' said Tyce.

'Not last, before they go home?' said Richard. 'What do you think, Timothy?'

'Both,' said Timothy.

That seemed a good idea, but there was another problem.

'Who's going to provide it?' asked Richard.

There was a long silence. Timothy remembered what hard work it had been finding enough extra food even for one young flycatcher when Tyce had first arrived. Richard knew only too well about feeding many beaks. Tyce had only just learned to fend for himself.

'Actually,' Tyce said, 'I'm one of the guests, really, because I shall be going away.'

'Everybody,' said Richard, 'will bring their own.'

'Is that all right?' said Timothy.

'Well,' said Richard, 'if you don't agree, you had better start finding tea for the moorhen straightaway; then, of course, there are the swifts . . . and all that fluffy seedy stuff the goldfinches eat . . .'

'All right,' said Timothy. 'Everybody brings his own. How will they know?'

'I'll send the family out to tell them about the party, and they can explain about the food at the same time,' said Richard.

Richard's first brood, of twelve, were now almost fully-grown; and the second batch, nine of them, were getting quite good at flying. They all became very excited at the prospect of a party and flew up and down the riverbanks, inviting everybody they knew and quite a few that they didn't. Luckily they were too timid to approach the bigger birds, apart from the moorhen. She was such a familiar figure, foolish and kindly, that nobody was afraid of her.

She was so pleased to be asked that she rushed straightaway to the shingle bank, where she found only Timothy.

'There's going to be a party here,' she told him. 'Would you like to come?'

'Yes, please. At least, it's my party,' said Timothy.

'Then you must come,' said the moorhen. 'I'm sure you'll enjoy it.' She peered around the empty bank. 'There doesn't seem to be anybody else here,' she said. 'I wonder if we've come to the wrong place.'

'It's tomorrow,' said Timothy. The moorhen looked at him blankly. 'I mean the party's tomorrow. This is the right place.'

'I hope you're right,' said the moorhen. 'It wouldn't do at all to miss it, would it? I think I'll have a little look downstream.' She paddled away, her head thrusting back and forth in jerks. 'I'll let you know if I find it,' she called back.

By three o'clock the next afternoon, the stretch of shingle between the water meadow and the river was alive with small birds of every description. Each had brought enough food to last him for the afternoon, apart from the moorhen, who hadn't taken in the bit about bringing one's own meal. She lurched about among the chattering birds, leaving great wet trails behind her, until she found Timothy. 'It was today,' she said. 'Isn't it lucky? So glad you were able to find the right place.'

Richard had been busy organizing competitions. Most of them were suggested to him by birds who were good at some particular skill – Tyce had asked for a flycatching contest, and the kingfisher for one to see who could catch the most fish. The swifts asked for a flying race, and the lark thought it would be fun to see who could fly the highest.

Because most birds saw no point in competing against specialists in their own fields, the competitions would not have lasted very long if it had not been for the robin who had unknotted Julian. He was quite sure he was going to win every contest and entered for everything. In the flycatching event, he caught one fly to Tyce's forty-two and Binda's forty-three. Not unnaturally, in the fishing, he had caught nothing at all when time was called just as the kingfisher swallowed his eighteenth minnow. Wet but perky, he remarked, 'I reckon I'm going to be the champion; I've had a second or third in every competition' – which was true.

Richard decided it was time to call the competitions to a halt and asked the moorhen to give away the prizes, since she had not entered for anything, never having discovered what was happening until it was too late. She was very pleased and presented one of her own black feathers to each of the winning birds, and a white swan's feather, found on the bank, to the robin, for coming in second so often. She did her job very nicely, smiling at each winner and saying, 'Very clever, I'm sure,' to each one. At the end, she turned to Timothy, who stood empty-handed beside her, and said, 'Where do I go for mine?'

Timothy bowed to hide his confusion, and there, at his feet, shone a golden dandelion. 'A special one for you,' he said politely, and handed it to her with another bow.

The moorhen was delighted. She tucked it behind her wing so that it stuck up like an umbrella, and showed it to everyone she met. 'My prize,' she would say, 'for giving away the prizes. Specially for me. Isn't it pretty?'

After that, the little goldfinches performed a dance, and the swifts gave a demonstration of acrobatics. This was nearly a disaster, for as they swooped low and fast over the heads of the crowd, several birds panicked and dived for cover, and others flattened themselves against the shingle bank, and pretended not to be there. A young whitethroat fainted, and the moorhen ran squawking to the river, treading on a party of warblers on the way, and drenched the whole company with spray as she scuttered away across the water.

After calm was restored, the robin approached Richard and suggested that he amuse the crowd by telling funny stories. Everybody waited hopefully while he began twittering to himself and hopping backwards and forwards, making little bows to where he had just been. After a time, Richard muttered to Timothy, 'When's he going to start?' And a thrush whose hearing was very acute said, 'Hush! I think he has started.'

After five minutes, some of the younger birds began to fidget and to ask their mothers if it was time for another meal; the older ones were gossiping under their breath.

'Tyce,' said Richard, 'you must stop him. It was you who asked him to come.'

'How?' said Tyce.

'You'll just have to . . .' Richard was interrupted by a commotion in the middle of the river, immediately behind the robin. There were frightful squawks and gurgles, and turbulent waves eddied out from the centre of the disturbance and raced up the shingle bank. For a time, the robin, intent on his story, did not notice what was happening; but as his audience all began to stand on tiptoe, or flutter up in the air to get a better view of what was going on, he turned round to find out what the fuss was about.

Just as he did so, the centre of the commotion was swept, amid tremendous shrieking and gurgling, on to the bank beside him. It rolled out on the shore and turned out to be the moorhen, hopelessly entangled in a bit of old fishing net.

Having failed to hear what the robin was saying, she had bundled off into the river to look for her tea. She had plunged her head down into the mud and stuck it straight through the old net which was caught up on some weed, and every effort she made to free herself only made matters ten times worse. Gasping and spluttering, she lay on the bank in a sodden heap.

'Ah,' said the robin. He hopped briskly down the bank. 'Now, just lie still and don't fuss.' The moorhen rolled a despairing eye at him and groaned. The robin straightened one or two strands and considered the problem. 'Now, if one or two birds could just give me a hand – no, not everyone. There's a young fellow here who has had some experience – ah, there you are; Tyce, isn't it? Now, pull that piece; hold on to that; here we go. Niçe little problem, this.' Tea and gossip forgotten, the crowd hung on his every movement with breathless concentration. 'Take that strand, and untwist it sunwise. Just raise the wing a little, madam. Easy does it. Now the foot – the other one. No, keep still now. There we are – not so tricky as it looked. No injury, I hope, madam? Just a trifle upset. Mind if I keep this net? Might come in useful for a spot of practice.'

The moorhen wobbled to her feet, water streaming from her in every direction. Tyce stood back, puffing and blushing. The robin gathered the net up, and the audience cheered loudly.

The robin bowed right and left. 'Now,' he said, 'where was I?'

'Just about to have tea,' said Tyce promptly. 'The others are all starting,' he added.

'So they are, so they are,' said the robin. 'Ah well, remind me to tell you the rest of that story some other time. Perhaps you'll come over to the garden one day, and I could teach you a little more un-netting. You show promise.'

Tyce thanked him, but his mind was on other things. He had made up a poem to be recited at the end of the party. All afternoon he had been looking forward to this moment, and so he had not minded very much when Binda beat him in the flycatching competition. But now he did not feel so sure about it.

As the birds finished their tea, a solemn mood fell on the company: a sense of impending partings, of the tiredness of a long day nearing its end, of many summer joys behind and unknown winter fears ahead. Occasionally a yellow leaf floated down, herald of naked days to come; and the migrants, the swallows, and parent flycatchers would move restlessly and whisper a word or two to each other. The river sucked and gurgled; a breeze rustled among the leaves and was still again.

Richard got up on his rock. 'The last item today will be a poem by Tyce, recited by the poet,' he said.

All the birds turned towards Tyce, silently waiting. He took a deep breath and began.

Over the shadowy oceans,
Over strange forests and streams,
Sunlight and moonshine go with us
To the faraway land of our dreams.

Good-bye to the banks where we feasted,
Good-bye to the meadows and trees;
Through storm cloud and tempest we travel
Far over the tumbling seas.

Like motes in the sunbeam for number,
Like star specks that spatter the sky,
We pass between cloud-piercing mountains,
Through sandstorm and sea storm we fly.

Good-bye to wood, orchard, and farmland,
Good-bye to the hedgerows and streams;
We leave you till spring melts your snow-shroud;
We fly to the land of our dreams.

By headland and hilltop we steer us,
Through desert and moorland we stray,
Strange cities and countries to greet us,
And homeland long sad seas away.

Good-bye to our friends by the river,
Good-bye to the dearest of streams;
We leave you to brave the ice-peril
And fly to the land of our dreams.

There was a little silence. Richard hopped on to his rock, and said, 'That is the end of the party. We hope you have enjoyed yourselves.' He stopped to clear his throat. Then he went on, louder. 'I should like to take this opportunity to wish a safe journey to all of you who will be leaving us in the next few weeks and to say that we look forward to seeing you again in the spring.' He knew, and they knew, that they would not all come safely home next spring.

Nobody was in a hurry to go. The sun went down behind the hills, and a pool of shadow fell on the shingle bank. The migrating parents began to discuss departure dates, and residents like Timothy and Richard and the robin thought about stoking up during the golden days that remained, to give them strength to live through the winter.

Suddenly a whirring sound made them all look up. A flock of swifts swung across the sky, calling to each other in their strange gypsy language. Jake and Liza crouched low for a moment on a ledge, wings tense and trembling, making soft guttural sounds in their throats. Then they lunged forward and swept away and upwards to join their fellows.

'Good-bye!' called the birds on the bank.

'Good-bye!' The swifts' reply dropped thin and piercing from far up the valley. Once they circled and flew over the assembled company.

'Good-bye!' cried Fleur, small and gold-bright on a thistle-head. The swifts hurtled by her, saluting her with flickering wings. Then they sped away, their calls growing ever fainter.

A trickle of conversation flowed among the guests. One by one, they said goodnight and slipped away into the gathering twilight. The robin escorted the moorhen home. She was crying freely into the river.

'It's the shock,' she said. 'And that poem – it was so sad.'

At last only Richard and Timothy and Tyce were left.

'It's my turn to say good-bye,' said Tyce.

'But you're not going *now*,' said Timothy, startled. 'Not *really* going.'

'Tomorrow morning, early,' said Tyce. 'There's a change in the weather. Fewer flies. We're going to sleep down at the bottom end of the valley tonight and be away first thing in the morning.'

'Tess and all?' asked Timothy.

'Yes.'

'Come back in the spring.'

'Yeth – yes.'

'Are you sure you'll find the way?'

'Of course.'

'How?'

'I don't know. I just will.'

Timothy understood that. 'Good-bye, then,' he said.

'Good-bye.' And Tyce flew away across the darkening meadow.

Timothy swayed on a stone for a long time and watched the pools under the bank grow blacker.

'Richard!' he called. 'Where are you?'

A small brown shadow slipped out beside him.

'I'm here,' said Richard.

7 The Storm

The summer visitors were all gone. The last dun leaf dangled from the alder bough, and dead grass, trailing in the river, trapped rafts of dirty foam where the current swirled under the tree roots. Colour was drained from meadow and hillside; only the ploughland glowed red.

It was the middle of November. Food was not exactly scarce, but difficult to find. Timothy could no longer bask on his stone and snap a casual meal from the clouds of midges that danced by, nor enjoy standing knee-deep in the cool water. The river ran high and green and cold, and it was better to peck about for snacks in the clammy earth.

Mist settled in the valley. For days it clung there, blotting out the hills, the farm roofs, even the far bank of the river; the willows loomed like pale ghosts. It crept under Timothy's feathers, and he felt perpetually moist and chilly. Wandering along the bank, he came upon Richard, busy as usual.

'I hate this weather,' he remarked.

'Oh, it's not so bad,' said Richard. 'All this mist gives me a safe feeling. It's better than snow.'

'I almost think I'd prefer snow. At least you can see where you're going.'

'That's silly. Nothing's worse than snow, unless it's really hard frost. At least you can eat in this weather.'

'I wish the sky wouldn't come down and sit on my head,' said Timothy. 'Do you think it will be sunny up on the hills? Perhaps they stick out of the top, like my stone sticks out of the water.'

'Go and see,' said Richard. 'You've been up there before, haven't you?'

'Never to the very top,' said Timothy. He thought about those barren slopes above the bracken line, the scented turf, the lichen-coated rocks. 'I think I will go,' he said. 'Just for a day or two. I might get to the very top this time.'

'Rather you than me,' said Richard. 'I'm a hedgerow bird, and it's no use pretending I'm not.'

Timothy set off the next day, stopping continually to snatch mouthfuls of food. No full, rich meals and then long hours dozing in the sunshine in November, but peck, peck, peck all the time to keep hunger at bay.

He dropped over the wall by Tyce's fallen tree and was on the open hillside. He prodded about in the mosses by a mountain stream, but dusk was already falling, so he spent that night close by the wall in a hawthorn tree.

The next day he went on up the hill. It was still damp and dank, but here the mist, instead of hanging in the air, seemed to be always falling in a fine drizzle. The sky grew a tone lighter.

'If the cloud keeps falling down, and I keep climbing up, then some time I must come out above it,' he thought.

He did. Late that afternoon, the shreds of mist fell below him, and he saw curve and bluff rearing out of the fog like a horse. Away to the left, a blot of sunlight fell on to the moor where a sunbeam had butted a hole in the cloud. The sunlight gradually shifted up the hill towards the peak, and Timothy followed it. Soon, weak and pale, it was shining on his pied coat.

For three days Timothy fed and slept on the mountain-top. He was not alone. The hardy pipits burst piping from clumps of whin, and the thin mountain sheep wandered everywhere, their fleeces pearled with dewdrops. Crows flung dark shadows across the turf, and sometimes a raven or a buzzard passed overhead, but nobody paid him any attention.

On the fourth day, a sudden eddy of wind pounced out of the stillness and flattened the withered grass; then it was gone. Timothy went on running about, pecking and bobbing. Then came another gust, a harder one. Timothy, caught unaware, nearly lost his balance. His long tail blew sideways, so that he could see it out of the corner of his eye without turning his head. He swung round and faced into the wind, and his feathers clung along the line of his body, from his beak to the tip of his tail.

At first Timothy merely felt excited at the stir of a new spirit on the hillside. This was a fine, free, brave life – far better than creeping about in the mist down in the valley.

Then there was a sudden hush, and he became aware of the emptiness around him. Not a sheep was in sight, not a pipit; the crows and buzzards had dropped down into the valley. Even the spiders and striped beetles among the whinberry bushes seemed to have slipped away into whatever crevices they could find. Timothy shivered. Perhaps he, too, ought to find shelter.

But it was too late. Without warning, the tempest roared across the stones and whistled down the slopes. Timothy crouched and faced it, every muscle straining to hold himself against the ground. He hardly dared to breathe, for fear the wind would blow him out like a balloon and toss him from moutain-top to cloud-top and away into space. Then it eased for a moment, and he straightened up, peering round for some sort of shelter. But a second gust leaped out at him and tumbled him over the moor, twisting his long wing and tail feathers so that he could not steer. The hillside fell away from him, and a new world of peaks and storm-swept plains unfurled beneath him.

'I must stop!' he cried to himself, and he tried to dive

down towards land. But a paw of wind patted him back up to his former height.

How long the world bowled by beneath him, he could not tell. But then the wind dropped as suddenly as it had sprung up, and he fluttered to the ground, battered and exhausted.

During his helter-skelter flight, he had been driven at least two miles beyond the mountain on whose slope he had been feeding. He was in a strange world, where the valleys all ran the wrong way, and no familiar river wound in the plains below him.

Instinct made him turn and work his way wearily back towards home – the same instinct which one day would bring Tyce faultlessly back to the single bank that he had left half a lifetime and half a world away. Although it would have been so much easier for Timothy to slip down into the shelter of the next valley, he pressed ever upwards, fluttering from rock to rock and keeping to the lee side of the peak so as to get some shelter from the blustery upper air. The wind had lessened, but the storm was not over. Instead of the smooth, grey sky of the past few days, the clouds were like rags tossing across a sea of blue; but all the time, the dark rags piled up, and the blue patches grew smaller.

Timothy cast an anxious glance at the storm clouds gathering, and pecked feverishly for food, for he did not know when he would be able to eat again.

Once he had reached the top of the shoulder and could see his own river below him, for the mist had been driven away by the wind, he felt happier. But now he was back on the windy side of the hill, and he moved cautiously, for he did not want to be caught a second time.

A few specks of rain were flung against him; the lower end of the valley was swallowed up in a haze as the main storm approached. The drops came faster, heavier, driven by the gale moaning in the gullies. Soon he was soaked through.

The very weight of his sodden feathers made it less likely that he would be blown away, but also made it impossible for him to fly.

Winded, soaked, bruised, half-stunned, he lay on the bare hillside, powerless as a shred of seaweed. Occasionally tail or wing feather flapped up in the wind, but the torrent of water pouring from the sky pinned him to the ground. Once he tried to raise himself and was immediately half-thrown, half-rolled up the slope until checked by a jutting rock. It gave no shelter from wind or rain, but at least it was an anchorage.

Darkness soon fell, but the storm raged long into the night. The rivulets leaped shouting over the rocks like wild beasts, and clumps of grass, loosened by the flood, blew along the slopes. The whole hillside streamed with running water.

Before dawn, the storm had spent itself. The ragged clouds lay strewn about the sky, but stars appeared between the rifts. A still, white moon slid into a clear patch and lit up the mountainside, shining on turbulent streams frothing into the valley below, wet rocks, and uprooted clumps of whin and heather, and picked out, beside a jagged boulder, a heap of black-and-white pulpy feathers huddled there.

Next morning at sunrise, Richard stretched on his alder twig down in the valley and burst into song. Then he looked about him.

The river frothed by; wisps of grass, twigs, leaves, Wellington boots, old kettles, a child's plastic trumpet, pieces of timber tumbled along in its current.

'What a night!' said Richard. 'Thank goodness that's over. I wish Timothy was back.'

Ruth slipped up beside him. 'Do you think he is still up there?' she asked. 'It was bad enough down here; I thought our tree would be blown into the river.'

'Can't do anything about it till we've eaten,' said Richard, searching busily.

Ruth watched him for a moment. 'I suppose that means you're going to look for him,' she said.

'Yes,' said Richard. 'I suppose I am.'

Twenty minutes later, he flew up the river and followed the line of the hedge up to the lane, crossed it, and went on to Tyce's fallen tree. There he rested. He had never flown as far as that before.

He took a quick second breakfast and flew on, over the wall. The dead bracken had been beaten flat by the storm. Richard would have preferred to flit up in the shelter of the stems, but though he could creep short distances through the cave-like undergrowth, he could not go far without coming up against a swathe of sodden fern blocking his path. He gave up the attempt and flew, unwillingly, over the top. Soon the bracken thinned away, and he was left on the bare hillside.

He did not care for this open ground at all, but there was no help for it. Sometimes a stunted thorn or a rock gave a little shelter. Then he came to the first thin clumps of whin and the occasional patch of heather. He began to look about him.

'Perhaps,' he thought, 'Timothy is hereabouts.' He puffed out his feathers and sang – a strange, piercing call on the silent moorland.

A wet sheep blundered past him, snatching at the short grass. As he listened to the stillness after his last long three notes had died away, he heard only her urgent tearing at the turf and the rustle of a beetle climbing a whinberry bush. He called again, but there was no reply.

On up again. The ground sloped more steeply; now there were only withered grass and stones all the way to the top, far above him.

It was not a blowy day; the wind had died down in the night. But there are always currents of air up on the hills that valley dwellers know nothing of, and Richard, feeling his feathers ruffle, felt alarmed. He looked for shelter, but there was none. He stared back down the way he had come and saw the silver thread of the river far below. How narrow it looked, and how small the patch of green that was the wide water meadow! Already he was tired out. He wondered how he was going to make the return journey with Timothy – or without Timothy.

He called again. He longed for hedges. Suppose a hawk comes over; where should I hide?' he thought. But when a kestrel did appear soon afterwards, Richard did the right thing by instinct. He flattened himself motionless against the turf. He could imagine the winnowing wing-beats as the hawk hovered overhead, the downward plunge of the head – scanning the bare ground for living creatures, the strong talons hanging down ready to grasp and tear, and the fierce yellow-rimmed eye, searching out every crack and hollow on the exposed hillside.

But Richard was a very small bird, and very brown, and the hillside that morning was full of small brown patches where wind and water had torn up grass, dislodged stones, tossed up leaves from the valley below. The kestrel hung there a little longer, and then a few sweeps of his wings carried him over to another hunting-ground.

As long as he remained in view, Richard dared not move, and even after he had disappeared into the next gully, the wren lay low.

At last he rose and shook himself. 'Hmmm,' he said. 'A nasty fright, that.' He toiled on up the hill, thinking how much easier his search would be if he had eyes and wings like a kestrel. Then a fearful thought struck him. Suppose the kestrel had found Timothy?

He called again. His voice sounded weak and trembly in that great expanse. The only other sound to break the silence was the harsh croaking of some crows heading over the mountain and quarrelling as they went. Richard did not

mind them. A crow might take a fledgling or an injured bird, but it would not attack a grown, healthy one, however small.

He watched them fly over, tumbling and cawing. Then one dropped to the ground near the ridge, flew up again once or twice, cawed, and hopped forward again. The other crows, in ones and twos, wheeled down out of the sky and joined him. They formed a semi-circle near a jutting boulder. Every now and again, one would go nearer, croaking; then all the others would go nearer too.

Richard moved a little closer, but not too close. He did not care for the creatures, with their hard, black beaks and strong feet.

Once he had seen them grouped like that around a sickly lamb in a field by the river; he had been glad when the farmer strode over to pick up the lamb and the crows, disgruntled, had flapped away. It could not be a lamb now, in November; anyway, the patch of shadow below the rock could only hide something much smaller than a lamb.

At once, Richard knew what it was. Straight up the steep hill he flew, swearing with shrill, angry notes as he went.

'Titititititititic!' he shouted. 'Tic! Tic! Tititic!' How often he had mocked a daytime owl with the sound. Now he spat it out with all the fury and power he could muster 'Tititititititititic! Tititititititititic! Tic! Tic Tic!'

Now he was among the crows, flicking his stumpy tail, turning himself about, darting first at one great bird, then another.

One crow hopped back, startled, as Richard flew at its face. Another made a lunge at the tiny wren, but Richard buzzed about its head till it spread its great wings and flapped a few paces off. Richard was back at a third, who swung its head about, trying to avoid the fluttering wings, jabbing at its tormentor with its huge beak, but always too slowly.

Richard could do them no harm, but they were no match for him in speed and agility, nor in the burning fury of his courage. For a minute they conferred, squabbling, on a patch of ground a few yards away. Then they rose up and wheeled off over the brow of the hill.

Richard, breathing hard, turned back to the boulder. Out of the corner of his eye, during his attack on the crows, he had seen the flecks of white. Timothy lay there, he knew.

'Hey, Tim,' he whispered. The wagtail half raised his head and stared dazedly. 'It's me – Richard. Are you all right?'

Timothy gave a broken twitter and let his head fall back on the ground.

Richard watched the wet bundle for a moment. A shiver rippled under the pied coat. The wren nudged the cold body into a nook in the rock and squatted down against it. After his headlong flight up the hillside, and the temper and energy expended on the crows, Richard was glowing with warmth. He was not sorry to rest, either; but as the minutes passed and the chill seeped through his feathers where he leaned against the sodden wagtail, he began to get fidgety.

'Timothy?' he said, and he moved away to look at him. At once Timothy slid limply down the slope, wings drooping. Richard shoved him up again and crouched the other way. He waited, staring down towards the valley so far below.

The crows passed overhead again, but they seemed to have forgotten Timothy, for they sailed straight on and out of sight. A spider climbed across the grass stems a few inches away, and Richard watched it longingly.

Suddenly he felt a movement beside him. He squinted sideways and met Timothy's beady black eye close to his own. Cautiously he sidled an inch or so down the slope. Timothy began to slide after him, but then he put out one leg and stopped himself. Flat on the ground, one wing trailing, the other folded awkwardly beneath him, Timothy stared at Richard. 'Chittip?' he said.

'Hmmm,' said Richard. 'You look like a dying duck in a thunderstorm. Would you like something to eat?'

'Yes. No. I don't know,' whispered Timothy. He laid his head down again, but he kept his feet braced against the ground.

'I'll see what I can find.' Richard searched for grubs, always keeping one eye cocked in Timothy's direction. After a time, he returned with a beakful. Timothy pecked very feebly at first, but when Richard came back with a second helping, the first had all disappeared.

For about an hour, Richard fed and kept watch while Timothy dozed uneasily, shivering a good deal. His feathers were still very wet, and when a weak sun began to shine, Richard shoved him down the slope out of the shadow. 'Now,' he said, 'stretch your wings out.'

Timothy was so stiff that every move was painful. However, he slowly forced his wings out over the grass and sat there, head sunk between his shoulders. At first he felt colder than ever, as the wind blew through his damp feathers; but gradually as they dried off and the pale sun penetrated to his skin, he began to feel more like himself.

'We shall have to start thinking about shelter for the night,' said Richard. 'Do you think you can fly?'

Timothy fluttered his wings a little. 'I ache,' he said, 'all over.' He staggered forward a few steps and then sank down exhausted.

'Never mind,' said Richard. 'You stay here and I'll see if I can find a shelter not too far away.' When he came back a few seconds later, Timothy was attempting to preen his feathers.

'That's right,' said Richard. 'Now I've found a good place just over the gully. Can you get that far?'

With a good many rests and much encouragement from Richard, Timothy eventually managed to make the journey. In the next gully stood some old dry-stone walling – probably the remains of a sheepfold. The rocks had fallen higgledy-piggledy, and Richard had discovered a miniature cave made of two or three flat stones. The entrance was just wide enough for a wagtail, and inside it opened up to a width of five inches. There they spent a warm, dry night, and by morning Timothy was well again.

It took them three days to get home, for both birds were tired and had to stop often to find food.

For the first two nights after they returned, Timothy slept long and late, getting back his strength. But on the third day, he woke earlier than usual. He heard the perpetual ripple of the river; he knew, without opening his eyes, the exact pattern of twigs he would see silhouetted against the sky; he felt the rough curve of the branch under his feet. This was home. And this morning, as for each morning since he got home, he felt that special sense of delight that comes from knowing a great danger is past.

All the same, there was something different in the air this morning, and when he opened his eyes, he knew what it was. The light was different – clearer, paler; it was this that had awakened him. He looked up at the hills where he had lived through the storm and saw they rose up white and still – rank upon rank of gleaming peaks.

'I thought so,' he said. 'Snow.'

There is always something special about the first fall of snow. Timothy knew it was unlikely to fall in their valley until the new year, but even so, those white hills marked the start of a new season. Autumn was over, and winter had arrived. Now the struggle for survival was on in earnest. But winter, hard though it was for small birds to endure, held the seeds of happiness in a way that autumn, with its shortening days and falling leaves, did not. For now the days would lengthen again, and every hard day endured meant a step nearer spring.

'I wonder if Richard has seen the snow up there,' Timothy said to himself. 'I must go and tell him.' He flew off down the river to find his friend.

8 Busy Times

Although snow first fell on the hills in November, it did not come to the valley till well into the new year, and it hung on until late February. Then one day Timothy noticed a dark line running across the snow-covered water meadow, marking the course of the ditch. It had been invisible for weeks, but now he could see mud and a thin trickle of water. He dropped down and found that the edges of snow were creeping back and revealing green grass.

He ran up and down, feeling the good earth between his toes and smelling the rich smells of vegetation. He prodded his beak into the soil – still bone-hard under a thin layer of mud. He splashed in the trickle of water – but not for long, because it was cold with melted snow.

Timothy was thin; for though he had spent the last months feverishly hunting for food, he had usually gone to bed hungry. All the same, he had just finished his spring moult and looked smart in a new glossy suit.

He watched a patch of snow glistening in the sunlight. A moist crust formed on the surface; the edge gleamed and then, as a drop formed, glittered in all the colours of the rainbow. Timothy blinked at the brightness. The drop grew and broke away, and a new one began to form in its place.

Birds were everywhere. A flock of starlings fed on the sunny side of the field, where the snow had shrunk to so thin a crust that they could thrust their beaks through into the ground; and wherever they waddled, they left dark footprints.

A party of fieldfares straggled overhead, calling to each other, and dropped down on the other side of the hedge from the starlings. They fed urgently, but not rudely like the starlings. Timothy settled near them.

'Good feeding this morning,' he remarked politely to the nearest bird.

The fieldfare raised his head and let his eyes rest on the distant hills. He was rather like a thrush, only greyer and slimmer.

'The change of the season,' he said. 'We must be leaving soon.'

'Why do you always go when the best time of the year is coming?' asked Timothy.

The fieldfare was feeding again and did not answer at once. Then he said, 'Tell me about it.'

Timothy thought for a moment. 'The leaves come and grow thicker and thicker; insects hatch out in thousands, and there are clouds of them hanging above the river. Sometimes the sun shines for weeks on end, and the earth gets dry and dusty; then the rain comes, and the earth whispers and mutters as it soaks it up, and it smells – oh, I can't tell you how glorious it smells. Then everything begins to grow, and the water meadow is full of long grass and kingcups, and the cows come down there – all warm and steamy from the milking-shed.'

The fieldfare stared into the distance again. He had a habit of doing that, like someone used to wide horizons. 'I shouldn't like that,' he said. 'When the celandines flower, I begin to think about the pine forest in Norway. I want to stretch my wings and fly away from all this, over the grey sea. We all get the same feeling. We begin to think about our other home, and nests, and young ones. We wake and call to each other in the early morning and late at night; and one day, we all rise up and go.'

He called now, throatily, 'Cha-cha-cha-chack.'

A nearby fieldfare stirred and half fluttered his wings, glancing up from his feeding to stare, too, at the hills.

Timothy moved on downstream.

A great-tit sat on an alder tree and sang his saw-sharpening call notes to greet the spring. 'See-saw-see-saw-see-saw-see-saw-see-saw.' He paused for breath and saw Timothy. 'First time I've sung that this year,' he said. 'That's why I'm a bit husky.'

'I always look forward to hearing you start the season off,' said Timothy.

'Ah,' said the great-tit. 'I know. They all do. I do myself. But some days are singing days, and some are not. I can't make myself sing.'

'Today's singing day,' said Timothy.

'You're right,' said the great-tit. He cleared his throat and began again. 'See-saw-see-saw-see-saw-see-saw-see-saw.'

Timothy left him and went on his way, but from far down the valley he could still catch the shrill *see*. And though the lower *saw* escaped him, he could fill in the gap in his mind.

He passed over a field of kale where fat pigeons feasted, and over the hedge busy with flocks of chaffinches and yellowhammers. He had decided to go and call on the robin in the garden of the big house.

On the shady side of the rhododendrons, the snow still lay deep. Timothy flew over them and on to the chimney where Tyce had once been mobbed by sparrows. There were no sparrows there now, but when Timothy ran round the far side and looked over the jumble of roofs, there they were, chasing each other up and down the slopes from which the snow had slid down into the gutters. A piece dropped off and fell with a slushy *plop*, and the sparrows broke off their endless games to peer over the edge. Then they started again.

Timothy flew off to the kitchen-garden wall. Here, too, the snow lay smooth and white on the shaded side. Some tall brussels sprouts leaned sideways over the snow. Water dripped from a pile of pea-sticks in the corner. Timothy minced along the top of the wall, finding food in the cracks in the coping and enjoying the feel of the sun on his feathers.

Then he heard the robin sing. He looked about him but at first could see nobody. Then what he had taken to be a russet leaf bobbed and turned into a small brown bird who flew quickly to the ground, picked something up, returned to his perch, bobbed, swallowed, bobbed again, and sang another verse. Timothy flew across and joined him.

'Ah,' said the robin. 'The dancing gentleman. How d'you do?'

'Very well, thank you. How are you?'

The robin ignored this, as one who is never ill. 'You've lost weight,' he said severely. 'Not been looking after yourself properly.'

'I've tried,' said Timothy meekly. 'It's not easy in the winter.'

'Nonsense. Just a matter of organization. I never go short. Human beings, you know. Mind you, I don't altogether care for their food – too starchy. But there's usually plenty of it if you're there at the right time, and you can always make up the meaty side of it if you keep an eye on the digging. Trouble is, when it's really frosty, they don't dig. However, I have other strings to my bow.'

He dropped down and pecked at the melting edge of snow. 'My mistake – thought I saw a grub. Then there's the house. I know most birds get a bit panicky about going indoors, but it doesn't bother me. There're always flies in the window cracks, and the humans often leave great hunks of stuff about. I steer clear in the ordinary way, of course, but needs must when the devil drives.'

'It's more pleasant when he doesn't,' murmured Timothy.

'Like to hear me sing?' Without waiting for an answer, the robin flung up his head and trilled. 'I know my stuff is not considered of a very high standard,' he remarked, 'but it gives pleasure to a lot of people, especially in the winter when no one else is singing. Now a blackbird has a lovely voice, I grant you, but he won't think of singing unless the weather is just right, and the time of year, and so forth. I just keep going, whatever I'm feeling like – my public expects it.'

'Humans?'

The robin nodded. 'They do a good bit for me, one way or another.'

A blackbird hanging about in a nearby pear tree caught the robin's eye and hopped over. He dropped a worm at the robin's feet, glanced at Timothy with some embarrassment, and flew off chuckling.

'Thanks!' called the robin after him. 'I've got an arrangement with that chap,' he remarked. 'Comes in handy at this time of year.'

He jumped up on to a wheelbarrow handle. He looked a little ragged, but very erect. 'The hard times are over for another year. There's a lot to think about in the next couple of months. We shall be having that little fellow back – what's his name – Tyce.'

'Yes, I know,' said Timothy. 'I've been thinking about that.'

A dog bounded down the path, followed by a bent man with a spade. 'I must be off,' Timothy said quickly, and he swooped up on to the wall. He stopped there, watching the man turn over the dark earth where the snow lay thinly. The robin, who had flown into the apple tree when the dog first appeared, returned to the wheelbarrow and sang. The dog sat and watched. The old man dug steadily for a few minutes; then he stooped and picked something out of the soil and threw it on the ground by the wheelbarrow. The robin dropped like a stone, picked it up, swallowed it, bobbed, returned to the wheelbarrow, bobbed again, and began another song.

Timothy flew back to the river. He fed on the patch of shingle, barely showing at this time of year, and made his way upstream. Once a loud scuttering under some overhanging trees made him shoot up in fright, but it was only the moorhen who burst out and swam in circles mid-stream.

'How are you?' called Timothy, perching on the bank.

'Oh, I'm so glad you're back,' said the moorhen.

'Back?'

'I heard you were lost up the mountains. I was so worried.'

'That was a long time ago, in the autumn. I've seen you since then.'

'How time does fly. I was very upset, you know. I cried.'

'Thank you,' said Timothy, hoping this was the right thing to say.

'When are we going to have another party?' asked the moorhen hopefully. 'I enjoyed the last one.'

'We'll have a welcome-home party, shall we?' Timothy bounced up in alarm as the kingfisher flashed by.

'There's going to be a party,' the moorhen called after him. 'Not what you'd call a sociable gentleman,' she added to Timothy. 'I've been saying good-morning to him for years, but he never answers. Not like that robin. Very polite and sympathetic, he was. Will there be prizes?'

'I think so, don't you?'

'And a special one for me?'

Timothy caught the distant notes of a wren's song. 'I'm sure there will be. I must go now. Good-bye.'

'Yes,' said the moorhen. 'Busy times now.' She swam off, head jerking, and Timothy went towards the song.

Richard was sitting on Timothy's stone; his own driftwood log had washed away in the winter floods. He was in full song, his whole brown body quivering with effort.

Timothy ran up quietly behind him and waited. Richard, suddenly catching a glimpse of swaying shadow on the stone, stopped dead, froze for an instant, and then dived for cover, chittering angrily.

'Did I make you jump?' asked Timothy innocently.

Richard hopped back. 'I was just imagining I was chasing a crow,' he said. 'Several crows, in fact. Big black ones.'

Timothy shivered, then felt the sunshine on his feathers and turned the shiver into a dance. Richard filled his lungs and sang again.

'Hmmm,' he said, when the last long notes had died away. 'Time to get going. Ruth has been talking about eggs, and I must start thinking about nests. I like to have several ready, just in case.' He pulled a piece of moss out of the bank and examined it thoughtfully before discarding it. 'Lots to do; lots to do. I like being busy.' He sang again, with a rippling chuckle in the middle when he saw he had made Timothy jump.

'Well,' he said. 'See you later. No time to dawdle now.' He disappeared into the undergrowth.

Timothy stayed on his stone. 'The summer birds will be coming back soon,' he thought. 'I expect they're like the fieldfares – their friends down South will ask them why they don't stop there, but they'll be remembering the river, and the meadow, and the farmyard. Perhaps Tyce will be thinking of me. And they'll fly and fly until they come over between the hills and see this valley, and that's where they'll stop. One day, when I'm just about the place, I'll suddenly see Tyce catching flies like he always did, and the swifts will come screaming across the sky, and there'll be goldfinches in the apple blossom.'

Rudyard Kipling
The Jungle Book 60p
The Second Jungle Book 50p

These are the famous stories about Mowgli, the jungle boy and Toomai, Rikki-Tikki-Tavi, Kaa, and the other animals who teach him the jungle lore.
First published in 1894 and 1895, these two books are just as unusual and interesting now as they were then.

J. W. Fortescue
The Story of a Red Deer 50p

Delightfully illustrated and full of the timeless appeal of all young creatures, here is a book to enchant every nature-lover. From downy-haired calf to heavy-antlered stag, the red deer, Lord of the Forest, meets the other wild creatures who inhabit the English countryside . . .
A touch of magic for every young reader.

Marjorie Kinnan Rawlings
The Yearling 70p

This famous book is the story of Jody and of his pet fawn Flag. Jody lives in the backwoods of Florida, and it is a hard but satisfying life of farming, fishing and hunting. But when Flag becomes a yearling life becomes more complicated for Jody.

John Steinbeck
The Red Pony 50p

This is the poignant story of a boy, Jody, who above all wanted a pony. It is the story of how he got it, and how it died . . . But Jody waited, hoped and prayed for another pony and, finally but tragically, he got it . . .

Anne de Roo
Cinnamon and Nutmeg 30p

When Tessa Duggan finds Nutmeg the kid and then Cinnamon the calf wandering alone in the bush near her father's New Zealand farm, she little realizes what effect they will have on her life. Read this exciting story set in the bush and find out what happens to Tessa and the two strays.

James Aldridge
The Marvellous Mongolian 40p

Tachi, a young stallion, is taken from the rugged mountains in Mongolia where he was born and sent to a nature reserve in Wales, but he escapes and starts the long trek back home. Peep, the gentle Shetland pony, goes with him. This remarkable story is told through the letters two children write to each other – Baryut from Mongolia and Kitty from Wales.